A Collection

of Prayers

Frank L. Ford

Compiled by Shirley M. Ford

Copyright 2015 Frank Ford
A Collection of Prayers

Published by Yawn's Publishing
198 North Street
Canton, GA 30114
www.yawnsbooks.com

All rights reserved. No part of this book may be reproduced or transmitted in any form, electronic or mechanical, including photocopying, recording, or data storage systems without the express written permission of the publisher, except for brief quotations in reviews and articles.

Library of Congress Control Number: 2015941174

ISBN: 978-1-940395-99-9

Printed in the United States

INTRODUCTION

Frank had many qualities that endeared him to people: his quick wit and infectious chuckle that warmed the hearts of all of those around him, but most of all it was his sense of place. His place growing up in the beautiful mountains of Hinton and the New River area in West Virginia and his place in God's love and care.

While serving in the United States Army he was stationed in Germany and lived in several areas in the United States after graduation from Concord College, Athens, West Virginia, but he never forgot what gave meaning to his life. He could be anywhere and still be grounded in his faith, which shines through in this collection of prayers. In his conversational style Frank had a gift for making God accessible while always showing reverence and praise for his creator.

Frank's roots were deep in the things that mattered: family, faith and a sense of belonging. His fresh insights as he traveled on his spiritual journey makes this book a valuable devotional guide for all of us who may have difficulty finding the precise words to express our faith. We are thankful that Frank, firm in his place in God's love, has given us these words.

He came to work for the company where I was employed in Ohio. I appreciated his honesty, caring, and ability to explain things in a manner that made the even the toughest things understandable. We married, raised a daughter and son, and shared a happy adventure in life for 49 years

Contents

All Things	1
An Anchor	4
An Old Friend	6
As It Is Written	8
Attitude	11
Beauty	13
Blessings	15
Burdens	17
But God	19
Citizenship	22
Communion Service	24
Decisions	26
December 26th	29
Direction	31
Discouragement	33
Emotions	36
Family	38
Father of Mankind	40
Go Ask	43
God's Grace	45
Heart	47
In Awe	50
Incarnation	55
Indecision	57
Independence	59
Like David	62
Listening	65
Little Things	67
Loving Father	70
Mercy	74
Mister God	76
Mothers	78

Obligations	80
One	82
Outgrowing	84
Poor In Spirit	86
Prayer	88
Prayer of Praise	91
Promises	92
Psalm 23	94
Resurrection	96
Separations	99
Serenity	102
Sermons	103
Thanks	105
The Cross	108
The Dash In Between	110
The Future	113
The Lord's Prayer	115
The Prince of Peace	118
The Robber	121
The Ugly Tree	122
Thou Shalt Not	124
Times That Try	126
Troublesome Times	128
Two Prayers	130
We Believe	132
We Live By Faith	134
Worship	136
Yourself	139

A Collection of Prayers

ALL THINGS

We know that all things work together for good to them that love God. To them that are called according to His purpose. My understanding of this statement has been as follows:

All adversity in my life will somehow, at some time, work together for my good. It seemed to say that the tests, the trials, the troubles, are the means to an end. The idea is that on the other side of troubles, at some point in time, all adversity will have worked together and will have come to an end and the result of it is the good. One writer points out that what is to us the means to an end is to God the end itself – that His purpose is not later – it is now.

C. S. Lewis said, "God, who foresaw your tribulation, has specially armed you to go through it, not without pain, but without stain." Job went through it. Not without pain; he wished he had never been born. But he went through it without stain. The Bible says, "In all this, Job sinned not nor charged God foolishly."

I believe a one-word definition of life is struggle. The struggle is to contend with - to fight whatever would defeat us. I don't believe it's important to God how well off I come out of the struggle. I believe it's important how, and how well, I struggle. What was Job's adversity about? About having his sons and daughters and animals restored? Was that the good that all things worked together for? Or was it about Job, in the midst of it, saying, "Though He slay me, yet will I trust Him?"

I've come to believe the central issue in times of adversity is not "Where is God leading in all this?" The issue is that God is leading and I'm to follow, whether He is leading to another calling, or a different point of view, or even if He is leading in a circle and I end up just where I started. All this should be of no consequence to me. God's leading is to lead me to Him.

Father, forgive me for making myself the center of my thoughts. In doing so, I have manufactured in my mind the idea that Your purpose is to serve my desires. I have become a pretender to the throne.

Forgive me for allowing Satan to blind me so.

Your word tells me that my whole duty is to fear You, to love You with all my heart, soul, and mind, and to keep Your commandments. I have taken other duties upon myself – so many that this duty has been crowded into the background.

As the heavens are higher than the earth, so are Your thoughts higher than our thoughts. Help me, Lord, to remember that except for Your grace, I am only a worm and to remember that Thine, O Lord, is the greatness, and the power, and the glory, and the victory, and the majesty, for all that is in the heaven and earth is Thine. Thine is the Kingdom, O Lord, and Thou are exalted as head above all.

A Collection of Prayers

Help me to walk by faith, not by sight. Help me to trust when I don't understand, to follow as best I can when I don't know where I'm going, or why. Let my faith prevail where my understanding does not.

In the name of Him who works all things together for good. Amen.

Frank L. Ford

AN ANCHOR

Father, our prayer today is for an anchor. Something to hold to when so many winds blow us off course.

Winds of a way of thinking that condones personal satisfaction about all else.

Winds of change that come at a pace that almost makes us dizzy.

Winds of a knowledge explosion that ignores wisdom.

Many of us have come a long way from our beginnings, from learning of You at our parents' knee; from the insulation and comfort of our families; from when we first loved You and committed to walking with You.

We've grown, and learned, and become more deeply grounded. There are many lessons and truths that are no longer struggles for us. Still, there was a peace at the time of our beginning that seems to be more fragile, more elusive now.

The mindset we've adopted, where Christ's birthday is remembered and He is forgotten, seems to typify our world. Form is important, substance is forgotten – success is important, service is forgotten – growth is important, grounding is forgotten.

A Collection of Prayers

Father, we know the name of the Lord is a strong tower. The righteous run to it and are safe. We know that Jesus is our anchor and our faith is the chain that binds us to Him.

Forgive us for taking our eyes off of You.
Forgive us for allowing our courage to erode.
Forgive us for accepting the world's terms and conditions.
Forgive us for being silent just because no one seems to want to hear the truth.

Let us be honest; our world is not a rose garden. All is not right in our lives and putting on a "me too" face and going along with the crowd – any crowd – will not make it so.

Father, we need Your help. Father, we need You.
Help us to trust You more and our feelings less.
Help us to love You more and ourselves less.
Help us to believe You more and anything else less.

Nothing in our hands we bring, simply to Your cross we cling!

In the name of the One we serve. Amen.

Frank L. Ford

AN OLD FRIEND

I had occasion recently to spend time with an old friend. A friend from my childhood, many miles and many years from here and now.

It was a joy! I suppose it's a common experience in rediscovering a friendship, to marvel at how that friend has changed, only to realize that the change is in ourselves; the friend is the same.

Because of the experiences of the years, I see that friend differently; I hear differently, I feel differently. Because of this, I have a deeper understanding and deeper appreciation than I would have thought possible. That friend is also the friend of millions of others, and with all of us, to know more deeply is to love more deeply. That friend from my childhood is the Twenty-third Psalm. My experience has added meaning to the words that I memorized.

When I feel lost and alone, I remember that —
> You are my shepherd.

When I think of how I've wished for what is not, I'm reminded that —
> I shall not want.

A Collection of Prayers

When I am in turmoil and there is no peace —
> You make me lie down in green pastures.

When the storm waves of life are about to drown me —
> You lead me beside still waters.

When I am utterly dejected and discouraged —
> You restore my soul.

When I feel as though I have no value, no purpose —
> You lead me in paths of righteousness for Your name's sake.

When I doubt that You care for me in a personal way, I remember that —
> Though I walked through the valley of the shadow of death, I feared no evil, for You were with me.
> Your rod and Your staff comforted me.

When I think I have no worth in Your sight —
> You prepare a table before me in the presence of my enemies. You anoint my head with oil. My cup runs over.

It is such a joy, and relief, and comfort – a blessedness –
> To know beyond doubt that whatever my lot in days to come, surely goodness and mercy shall follow me all the days of my life. I will dwell in the house of the Lord forever.

Thank You, my Father, my Shepherd. Amen.

Frank L. Ford

AS IT IS WRITTEN

Paul wrote in the Corinthians, "As it is written, let him who boasts, boast in the Lord." That never sounded quite right to me, because I was taught that boasting was never good to do. As many times as I read this passage, it never occurred to me to look up the "as it is written" part. I assumed Paul wouldn't lie. If he said "as it is written," that's the way it was written. Then one day I found the "as it is written." It's in the book of Jeremiah and it's beautiful. Paul was not inaccurate, but he barely skimmed the surface. When we examine the "as it is written," there is revealed for us the mind and nature of God! Listen, as God speaks through Jeremiah.

> "Let not the wise man boast in his wisdom or the strong man boast in his strength,
> or the rich man boast in his riches, but let him who boasts boast of this; that he
> understands and knows Me, that I am the Lord who exercises kindness, justice, and
> and righteousness on earth, for in these things I delight, declares the Lord."

In the evening of the day that Jesus called Matthew, a tax collector, to be his disciple, He had dinner at Matthew's house. The Pharisees asked why Jesus ate with tax collectors and sinners. Among other things, Jesus told them, "Go and learn what this means; I will have mercy and not sacrifice."

If the Pharisees had gone to learn the meaning, they would have found it in Hosea – "I desire mercy, not sacrifice, and knowledge of God more than burnt offerings." If they had continued their search, they might have found that beautiful passage in Jeremiah.

Father, how appropriate are these passages at a season of thanksgiving. We thank You. We praise You because You delight in kindness, justice and righteousness. We see examples daily of power corrupting men – the more power, the more corrupt. But it's not so with You, Father. You have all power in Heaven and earth, yet You delight in kindness, and justice and righteousness.

Who among us has never boasted of their riches by feeling smug for being so well off? Who among us has never boasted of their strength by believing we have done for ourselves – our way? Who among us has not boasted of their wisdom in thinking that we're doing a pretty good job of directing our affairs?

And haven't we taken pride in how well we've done all these things? How many of us could boast that we understand You whose ways are as high above our ways as the heavens are above the earth? Forgive us, Father, for our foolish boasting.

Frank L. Ford

What good fortune; what blessedness it is for us that You delight in mercy, for we would surely perish without mercy.

We thank You for freedom in our land which we too often take for granted. We are a thousand times more grateful for the freedom we have through Jesus Christ. Because of His sacrifice, we are forever free of death and free of the dominion of Satan. Your truth has made us free indeed!

May we never again boast of our wisdom, or strength, or riches. May we ever reach, and strive, to practice kindness, justice and righteousness, and may we ever hold onto the hope of being able to boast that we know and understand You.

We ask all in His name. Amen.

A Collection of Prayers

ATTITUDE

I am your master. I can make you rise or fall. I can work for you or against you. I can make you a success or a failure. I control the way you feel and the way you act. I can make you laugh, work, and love. I can make your heart sing with joy, excitement, and elation or I can make you wretched, dejected or morbid. I can make you sick and listless; I can be a shackle, heavy and burdensome or I can be as a prism's hue – dancing, bright and colorful. I can be nurtured and grown to be great and beautiful, seen by the eyes of others through action in you. I can never be removed – only replaced.

I am your attitude.

The writer or Proverbs said, "Keep your heart with all diligence for out of it are the issues of life." Our attitude is one of the issues of life. I'd like to think that my attitude is my business. That I will determine whether I have a good or a bad day and that will be the end of it. But it's more; it is out of the heart; it is an issue of life.

Some people seem to always have a good attitude – I don't. I have moods and attitudes that I don't like, don't want, and can't control. But knowing that is not the answer. There is still the problem of changing. For that, I need help.

Father, thank You for being there to turn to. Thank You for

listening and for caring about our problem. And, thank You, Father, that Your love and power go beyond these things; that besides listening and caring You have the power and the will to help us make changes in our lives.

We wish our attitudes were private, that we could keep them to ourselves, but we can't do that. Attitudes are very contagious. We spread them to others. Fine, when we're spreading a good attitude, but shameful to have to admit that we must have spoiled other people's attitudes. We ask Your forgiveness.

Father, we know that Satan is very much involved in this matter. If he is not the cause of our negative attitudes, he is certainly the beneficiary of them. Help us to keep this before us. Help us above all not to serve Satan through carelessness or lack of attention.

We know that our attitude drives our actions, but we know too that the opposite is true. Our actions drive our attitudes. Make us diligent in serving, in doing for others, encouraging, complimenting, listening, and accepting graciously. All of these things and a hundred more can meet the needs of those we know – and our attitudes will benefit because of it.

Father, the problem is as subtle as it is important. We need Your help to be what You want us to be and what we want to be. Let us, above all else, guard our heart for it is the wellspring of life.

A Collection of Prayers

BEAUTY

Our children were growing up in the 70's – the age of Sesame Street – which began in 1969. That was also the era of the Muppets which figured prominently in the Sesame Street offerings. Like most people, we saw what our children watched, and we saw a good deal of Sesame Street.

One episode that has stayed with me was about a little boy who was separated from his Mother and cried because she was lost. Everyone tried to help him find her. They said, "What does she look like?" He said, "She's the most beautiful woman in the world." Everyone searched for the beautiful woman. They searched high and low, but no one could find her. Finally, she was found.

To everyone's surprise, she was not beautiful! She was, as my Mother would say, "Ugly as a mud fence." But she was beautiful to her son. He did what the Lord does – He looked at the heart and found beauty.

We were lost, and God found us. Not because He was looking for beauty. I wonder, how did He find us? I think He looked at our hearts and found such great need He was moved to compassion. Happily, God does not see as we see.

I was rambling around in Psalms and found this: "I am poor and needy, yet the Lord thinks on me." The idea is so overwhelming I had to read it again. . . and again.

Frank L. Ford

The Lord thinks of me. Let's pray.

Father, how puny and insignificant we are. How great Thou art! But wonder of wonders, we are not insignificant in Your sight. The Lord of the universe thinks about me – and those I love – all of us here now.

We are like the prodigal son who, when he came to himself, was ashamed of himself, but found, to his surprise and delight, that his father wasn't. Father, You chose us and You're not ashamed of it! All of us who are in Christ know this, and we all rejoice in it.

Come, Holy Spirit. Unite us in praising Your name and giving thanks for Your blessings. When we in awesome wonder consider all the worlds Your hands have made, and consider that You know us by name, who are a thousand generations removed from our beginnings, we bow in humble adoration and proclaim, "Oh Lord, my God, how great Thou art!"

Nothing in our hands we bring; simply to the cross we cling.
And there is nothing in our heart worth bringing to You.
As we realize and confess that we are nothing and have nothing, You give us everything!

Why should I mourn and toil within when it is mine to hope in God? I shall sing praise to Him; He is my help. He is my God. In Jesus name. Amen

A Collection of Prayers

BLESSINGS

I wish I had the eloquence to give to God the glory that is due Him, but I don't have the vocabulary necessary to remotely express the gratefulness for the good things in my life.

The gift of eloquent expression is only given to a few, but we all have the ability to count our blessings and say, "Thank You." Let's do that together for a few minutes.

Father, the first blessing we acknowledge is the blessing of prayer. By yielding our spirits, we are transported to Heaven in our mind and heart. We feel a comfort as real as being held in our mother's arms. You haven't set seasons or times. We may come to You in the best of times or the worst of times. Not only do You meet with us where we are, You patiently hear us and You give us the things we need. For this overwhelming favor Father, thank You.

We could not leave out the blessings of love. Your word tells us that You *are* love. In giving us the ability to love, You have made us like You. And we cannot leave out the joy of being loved – a blessing that we sometimes don't give adequate attention or appreciation. Let us pause and remember that family and friends – and You – love us, not for deeds we've done nor for what we are. They, and You, just love us. What a wondrous thing – how good it feels! What a need it meets. Thank You, Father, for love.

Among our greatest blessings is ministering. You have not

chosen to keep us in an ivory tower. You have allowed us to be subject to suffering, and sadness, and sickness, and death – subject to frustration, disappointment and despair. But whatever comes into our lives, You minister to us. You give us peace that passes understanding, and joy, and health, and life. You give us hope. You minister to our needs.

And You have given us the power to minister. We have the double blessing of being a blessing when we help others to grow, to feel good, and to do well. For ministering to our needs and allowing us to minister to other's needs, Father, thank You.

Father, we think of what we call the simple pleasures – things that please our senses. When we ponder for a moment, they are anything but simple. For five days, You created heaven and earth and all that is in them – wonderful things to see, to hear, to taste, to smell, and to feel. And on the sixth day, You made us – with senses to enjoy all that You had created – and to enjoy the man-made extensions of Your creations. Without these senses, our life would be bleak beyond our imagination. We could not see a sunrise, or a sunset, or a rose – we couldn't hear a baby laugh, or our favorite song – we would never taste our favorite foods – we would never smell things that carry us back in time to pleasant memories. We would never feel our arms around someone we love. For these simple pleasures, may we never take them for granted again – thank You.

Father, we know this a very short list of blessings. Accept our inadequate praise and thanks. We believe that one day, when we sing a new song to the Lamb, then we will be able to give to You the glory that is due. In His name, Amen.

A Collection of Prayers

BURDENS

The writer of Ecclesiastes says, "To everything there is a season and a time to every purpose under the sun." He also said, "I have seen the burden God has laid on men." Just as there is a time for everything else, there is a time for burdens. We have friends who are in that time now. Let us pray about burdens and those who carry them.

Father, at the urging of Jesus, we come to You in His name to talk to You about burdens and about our friends.

When burdens come we are usually, at first, overwhelmed. We're like Peter who was doing fine walking on the water, but when he saw the wind, boisterous – when he looked away from Jesus – he became afraid. Forgive our fickleness and self-centeredness. Then, after floundering and sinking, we find ourselves out of answers and afraid and decide we'll tell You about our burden – and realize, to our shame and relief, You've known about it all along and have been waiting for us to come to You as we've been taught to do.

We come to realize that the circumstances of our lives are ordained by You. By Your providence, You bring us into circumstances that we cannot understand – but You understand and Your Holy Spirit makes intercession for us.

We understand that You place burdens on us which You don't intend to lift off of us – You intend for us to give them to You. This must be what the Psalmist thought when he said, "Cast your burdens upon the Lord and He will sustain you." And why Jesus said, "Come unto Me all of you who are weary and burdened and I will give you rest. Take My yoke upon you and learn from Me for I am gentle and humble in heart and you will find rest for your souls."

We know that the Man of Sorrows, acquainted with grief, can understand how we feel and, praise God, cares because we feel that way. But knowing this does not take away the burden. Burdens aren't just taken away. We can't just turn away from them, or get around them, or over or under them. We must go through them.

We ask You to help our friends go through their burdens with grace and patience and faith – honestly desiring Your will, not their own. And give them peace – Your peace that passes understanding. The peace that mystifies us when it comes because we feel calm and at rest when there is no reason to feel that way.

Father, it is good to talk to You through Jesus who had burdens and understands. Amen.

BUT GOD

In the 1920's, Charles Evans Hughes, as Secretary of State, attended a Pan-American conference. He instructed his interpreter to give him a summarized translation of what was being spoken in Spanish or Portuguese, and said, "Give me every word after a speaker says the word "but." What follows "but" is of the utmost importance.

True as this is, it is much more true when God chooses to act in the affairs of men.

Let me call to mind a story we learned when we were young, then I'd like to offer a prayer and then will extend the prayer with a prayer written by Annie Johnson Flint.

The story of Joseph is a roller coaster ride. It is a story of tragedy and triumph. The tragedy of man's evil and the triumph of God's grace. It's a story we learned before we knew stories are history. Joseph was sold into slavery by his brothers – out of jealousy. When, by God's grace, he overcame when he was falsely accused of attempted rape and thrown into prison. Now he is in very deep trouble. He is in a prison, in a foreign land, without a friend and without hope.

The bible says, *"But the Lord* was with Joseph." But the Lord was with Joseph and showed him mercy and gave him favor in sight of the keeper of the prison.

After that, as you know, in time Joseph became second only to Pharaoh.

Later, when Joseph was reunited with his brothers who betrayed him, they cowered before him fearing their just punishment. He did not punish them nor even shame them. He had learned from God. He said, "You thought evil against me, *but God* meant it unto good." Let us pray.

Father, in so many times of trouble, of testing, of anxiety, You have been there for us. Not when we wanted You to be – but always there when we needed You to be. We remember being at the end of our rope – and at wit's end – *but God* had a way.

For some un-understandable reason we continue to live our life as if we were living it unchaperoned, unguided, and unprotected, as if we were alone.

We praise You because we are never unchaperoned, never unguided, never unprotected – and never alone! We praise You because of the, *"But God."*

In the words of the poet:

I know not, *but God* knows; oh, blessed rest from fear!
All my unfolding days to Him are plain and clear.
Each anxious, puzzled "why?" from doubt or dread that grows,
Finds answer in this thought: I know not, *but He* knows.
I cannot, *but God* can, oh balm for all my care!

A Collection of Prayers

The burden that I drop, His hand will lift and bear.
Though eagle pinions tire, I walk where once I ran,
This is my strength to know – I cannot – *but He* can.
I see not, *but God* sees, oh, all sufficient light!
My dark and hidden way to Him is always bright.
My strained and peering eyes may close in restful ease,
And I in peace may sleep; I see not – *but He* sees.

Amen.

Frank L. Ford

CITIZENSHIP

Father, as we pause to reflect on the anniversary of this, the country of birth for most of us and the country of choice for a great many, we thank You and praise You for this land, so richly blessed by You from its birth. We thank You that the founding fathers were consumed with the ideas of freedom and liberty.

And when we take this blessing for granted, as we do from time to time, let us remember Tiananmen Square, the Berlin Wall, and South Africa. There are many lands where men and women and children like us are not free to live where they want – not free to attend the school of their choice – not free to work where they want. We even have the freedom to desecrate the symbol of our freedom! Thank You that it is again popular to be patriotic. We can remember when patriotism was not in vogue.

Because of our experience in our time, we associate freedom with democracy. But we also live in a spiritual world, regardless of our flags or our borders. And our spiritual life is controlled by one of two absolute monarchs; one who is the true light, The Prince of Peace, and one who is the Prince of Darkness.

The Prince of Darkness was never elected – in his government, there is no legislature, no judiciary, and his subjects live in worse slavery than Hitler or Stalin or Deng in China ever imposed. These men could only control and kill the body. Satan enslaves and kills the souls of men and women.

Neither is The Prince of Peace an elected office. In His kingdom there is no legislature or judiciary. He is Sovereign but His subjects live free. He does not enslave; "The law of the Lord is perfect, converting the soul. The statutes of the Lord are right, rejoicing the heart; the commandment of the Lord is pure, enlightening the eyes. More to be desired are they than gold, yea, than much fine gold."

How thankful we are, Father, to enjoy freedom in Your service – to be free forever of the yoke of sin!

Because we are shallow, we often take blessings for granted. We forget that we live in a free land because our forefathers were willing to shed their blood to make it free. We forget that we enjoy spiritual freedom because Jesus was willing to shed His blood to make us free.

Father, help us in our resolve today to be better citizens of these United States of America and to be better citizens of that spiritual kingdom – which we were not born into – that kingdom which accepted us when we were aliens and made us joint heirs with its King!

Father, we bow before You in deep, heartfelt gratitude, respect, awe and admiration, acknowledging debts that we could never repay in a thousand, thousand years.

Amen.

Frank L. Ford

COMMUNION SERVICE

Last week, my friend gave me something she wrote and asked me what I thought of it. I liked it and decided it would be good to read as the beginning to the Lord's Supper. She had written:

> A small piece of bread, a small sip of wine,
> The value of each is priceless to mankind.
> The ultimate price was paid, so that every person could enjoy –
> Peace in trials,
> Strength in temptations,
> Comfort in sorrow,
> Forgiveness for wrongs,
> Guidance each day,
> Freedom forever,
> Grace to meet all our needs.

I continue with my thoughts:

Some 3500 years ago, God instituted the Passover Feast to memorialize the exodus of the Israelites from Egypt – their emancipation from slavery.

Some 2000 years ago, Jesus, while observing the feast with His disciples, instituted the supper that we're gathered for now.

This, too, memorializes an emancipation. But this one is an emancipation from the slavery of sin and it's for all people – whosoever will.

A Collection of Prayers

Prayer – Breaking of Bread

Father, as we eat the bread, accepting the sacrifice made for us, we give thanks for Your great love. Let us give our life not to its end, but in service for as long as we live. In Jesus' name.

Prayer – Cup of Wine

Father, as we drink the cup, accepting the sacrifice of Your life to pay the cost of our ransom, we do it with grateful hearts. In Jesus' name.

Prayer – The Offering

These gentlemen are here with the plates to receive our offerings. There are many reasons to make an offering – payback is not one of them. We can never repay what we've been given.

Let me suggest just one of the reasons to make an offering. It is in this building, or one like it, that was supported by the offerings of others that we heard and responded to God's calling.

The best we can do is pay it forward with our offerings so that in the future people will have the same opportunity we have had.

Thank you, Father, that You provide over and above our needs – always – enough to share with others. In Jesus' name.

Frank L. Ford

DECISIONS

Throughout the Bible, we find people faced with decisions.

From Genesis:
"You are free to eat from any tree in the garden, but you must not eat from the tree of the knowledge of good and evil."

From Joshua:
"Choose for yourselves this day whom you will serve, but as for me and my house, we will serve the Lord."

From Matthew:
"My Father, if it is not possible for this cup to be taken away unless I drink it, may Your will be done."

From Revelation:
"I stand at the door and knock. If anyone hears My voice and opens the door, I will come in and eat with him and he with Me."

Decisions, decisions, decisions! From Genesis to Revelation. Even a casual reader of the Bible must conclude that God's word does not provide answers to everything. A careful reader of the Bible must conclude that it isn't meant to. God intended for us all to make decisions, beginning with a decision about our soul and never ending.

Father, in Your wisdom, You have chosen to force us into making decisions. That wisdom escapes us when we are forced to make decisions that we don't feel adequate to make, and especially when we are forced to make decisions that we don't want to make.

We have all experienced making decisions that denied ourselves and others something. Decisions that hurt feelings. Decisions to let go of something precious. Decisions that we weren't free to explain or justify. We've learned that even right decisions often don't look right to others and, very often, don't feel good to us. We've learned that the best we can do is sometimes wrong and frequently an act of faith. Only time will tell whether we've made the right choice.

Father, You know that having to make hard decisions sometimes makes us feel alone – sometimes makes us subject to criticism, sometimes makes us feel inadequate, sometimes makes us resent being placed in the role of being the decision maker.

Knowing this, You have nevertheless placed us in that role. We must believe You did so to make us grow rather than feel good. You must have done it to make us accept responsibility and to become mature.

Thank You, Father, in this as in every area of our life. You have chosen the best way for us over the easy. And, as in every other area of our life, You have not left us alone. You have promised us wisdom, if we but ask.

Help us to accept the responsibility that You have placed on us to choose wisely, and to never forget that we need not be alone when it's time to make hard decisions. We have Your word for a guide, the counsel of our brothers and sisters and, above all, Your wisdom available to us as if it were our own.

Help us, O Lord, to trust in You with all our heart and lean not to our own understanding. May we, in all our ways, acknowledge You. We trust You, Father, to direct our paths.

Amen.

DECEMBER 26th

December 26th is the day our thoughts turn to taking down the tree and putting away the trappings of Christmas. Soon the day is forgotten and that's as it should be when we celebrate the holiday.

But when we celebrate the Christ, the celebration goes on. God is eternal.

Father, the prophet foretold that unto us — who are sinful and undeserving — a child is born. Unto us — who were hell-bound and without hope — a Son is given and He will be called Wonderful.

Father, You have called Him the Wonderful Counselor, the Mighty God, the Prince of Peace and as He is all these things to all mankind, He is to each of us — He is to me.

He is our Counselor,
- — Sometimes commanding,
- — Sometimes leading, sometimes prodding,
- — Sometimes giving insight,
- — Sometimes giving wisdom,
- — Always giving direction, in the most needed and most loving way.

He is our Mighty God, a fortress against the wear and tear of the world,
- — Against temptations,
- — Against discouragement and weakness,
- — Against all that Satan puts in our way to distract us, and lead us astray.

He is the Prince of Peace,
- — Who quiets hearts toiling with fear,
- — Who teaches love to hearts that envy and bear grudges,
- — Who strangely warms hearts that are breaking,
- — Who brings peace that passes all understanding.

Father, though we have heard this story all our lives, we still can scarcely believe that You so loved us that You gave Your only Son for us.

This is the miracle of Christ.

This is the greatest gift.

By Your grace, we continue to enjoy these gifts each day, all our lives. And beyond our life, we look for the blessed hope, the glorious appearing of the great God and our Savior, Jesus Christ.

Amen.

DIRECTION

Direction for our lives is a problem for many of us. On our journey on the King's Highway, we continually encounter detours, blocked roads, washouts and getting lost. Sometimes we're not even sure we're still on the highway. We're not even sure we know how to drive.

Jeremiah said,

> "O Lord, I know that the way of man is not in himself.
> It is not in man that walketh to direct his steps."

Father, we thank You for the love that fashioned a cross that brought us up out of a horrible pit, out of the miry clay, and set our feet upon a rock. And we praise You that You did not deal with us in half measures. Having rescued us, You put a new song in our mouths, even praise to our God.

Still, Father, we have a great need that we cannot fill. We believe that the grace that brought us to the cross is the grace that will direct our steps – all our lives.

Father, there is something in us that causes us, or lets us, to believe that we can adequately direct our lives. Help us to understand that this is not in Your will. Help us to understand that Your spirit indwells us for Your purpose, not ours.

We believe that we are instruments – that You do act through us, that You did not give us mouths to be muzzled, nor feet to mark time, nor brains to parrot traditions. Help us remember that we are only instruments – worthless alone, but capable of great things in the hands of the Master.

Help us to learn to yield ourselves to Your Holy Spirit. Let us measure success, not by how much we have done, but to how much we have relied on You.

Help us, O Lord, to trust in You with all our heart and lean not on our own understanding. May we, in all our ways acknowledge You. We trust You, Father, to direct our paths.

Amen.

DISCOURAGEMENT

Discouragement is something that we all wrestle with. The writer of Proverbs knew discouragement. He said, "Hope deferred makes the heart sick."

Discouragement is a debilitating, energy-draining feeling that is sometimes expressed by a feeling of "What's the use?" Or in the extreme, as in the 28th chapter of Deuteronomy, "In the morning you will say would God it were evening, and in the evening, you will say, would God it were morning."

Father, one time we believe that we're strong, and independent, and in control, and then become discouraged, and believe we are weak and helpless. We allow discouragement to blind and deafen us. It's as if we had cataracts that keep us from seeing the many good and positive things right in front of us – as if we wore ear plugs to shut out Your voice. It seems we only have eyes and ears for the negative. And when we've closed our eyes and ears and our heart, the devil says, "Now you see yourself as you really are." And we're not sure which self is real.

We know even Jesus felt discouraged by the lack of faith He found in Israel and in His disciples. We know He was discouraged when facing His trial, humiliation and death as He said, "Now is My soul troubled."

Frank L. Ford

Discouragement must surely be one of Satan's favorite points of entry into our lives. He is free to bring in a thousand other devils as long as we remain stalled and stagnated and focused on our dilemma or ourselves.

But Father, nothing is too small for You to hear and care about and nothing is too great for You to accomplish.

Help us to learn to weigh and evaluate the events and circumstances in our life from Your point of view rather than our own so we can see that our hopes are more important than our disappointments. That how we think is more important than how we feel; that what we hope for is more important than what we have.

Help us to see that Your grace is sufficient for discouragement, too. Thank you that Jesus, who said, "Now is My soul troubled," also said, "Let not your hearts be troubled." Thank you, Father, for hearing and caring.

In the words of the poet Annie Johnson Flint,

You give more grace when the burdens grow greater,
You send more strength when the labors increase,
To added afflictions, You add Your mercy,
To multiplied trials, Your multiplied peace.

A Collection of Prayers

When I have exhausted my store of endurance,
When my strength has failed ere the day is half done,
When I reach the end of my hoarded resources,
Your full giving has only begun.

Your love has no limit,
Your grace has no measure,
Your power, no boundary know unto men,
For out of your infinite riches in Jesus,
You give and give and give again.

Thank You that we may pray – in Jesus' name. Amen.

Frank L. Ford

EMOTIONS

Last week was one like few others in my memory. I can't remember when I was so glad to see a week end. I saw or was reminded of the hurt of death, the helplessness of being an invalid, the hurt of a careless remark, frustration with bureaucracy, the infliction of suffering through spite, unfairness and countless examples of stupidity. To be fair, I also saw and heard of examples of love, caring, praise, friendship, sharing, generosity, and sacrifice.

It was an emotional roller coaster. It left me drained. I don't think that my experience was unique. I know that all of us have had the same kind of week – if not last week, then some other week.

I thought perhaps there was some deep truth to be gleaned from this week spent as an emotional punching bag. But I couldn't pull from all of this a single deep truth – or even a half-deep truth. I did, after some thought, identify two simple truths: when bad things happen, or threaten, we should talk to God about it and, when good things happen, we should talk to God about it.

Father, I need someone to run to, someone to tell my feelings to, someone who cares about justice and fairness, someone who is angered by injustice, who can and will, one day, see that justice is done. Father, I'm thankful that I find all of these needs met in You.

I thank You that when Your people are grieving over death, You offer a peace that passes understanding – that You offer life that conquers death. You are a God that has known death – and resurrection.

I know from the book of James that You care about the harm and the hurt inflicted by the awful power of the tongue.

I know that You must be grieved when we misuse the intelligence You've given us for self-serving to undercut, and belittle, and create suspicion.

Father, I know, too, that You approve and reward when we act as Your word teaches that we should. I know that it's good for people to witness Your children showing love, practicing friendship, sacrificing for others, helping, and encouraging. I am so glad that You're a God who wants these things for Your people. I'm glad that meekness before You is not weakness. I'm glad for the strength and courage shown to help others. I'm gladdened to see people pay the cost to serve You by serving others.

Father, I know that many people who are experiencing the things I've talked about are seeking Your help and finding comfort and solace – and their needs are far greater than mine. I know that if prayers had to be important to be heard, mine wouldn't rise above the ceiling. But I know that You haven't imposed restrictions – that a sincere prayer in Jesus' name will reach Your ears. Thank You for hearing me too.
Amen.

Frank L. Ford

FAMILY

There is probably nothing in the world so valuable, and so taken for granted, as our families. When I was young, I had a father, mother, a sister and two brothers. I knew what a family was and I knew what our roles were: we were provider, homemaker, and students. We worked, we played, and sometimes stayed out of the way.

That seemed to be the whole story. I didn't realize there was something going on. I thought the family was an end in itself. I didn't realize it was a means to an end. I like to think that if I had realized how much I was involved in learning about life and about God, I would have paid closer attention. It never occurred to me that the family is God's way of demonstrating His love.

But in spite of myself, I did learn some things and that's what I want to pray about with You this morning.

Father, as we think of family and what it means to us, surely more than anything else it means unconditional love and acceptance. Only in the family do we not have to earn love and acceptance. We know we are loved even when we do not live up to expectations – when we fall or fail or even abuse our family's love.

In these things, Father, the family teaches us about You – about Your unconditional love – that You love without respect to person, that Your rain falls on the unjust also.

In the family is where we learned that unity is more important than uniformity, that harmonizing is worth more than synchronizing. In the family, there is room for being different and being loved in spite of it.

From this we learned that You too value unity over uniformity, that You accept us as we are – of many sizes, shapes, temperaments, and in many stages of imperfection. We learned that only You will decide what is clean and unclean. We learned that if You created such a variety of people and plants and animals, we may not build a wall around ourselves and our kind.

In the family is where we learned that where there are high standards, there is also mercy for falling short. We learned that not only do sons and daughters, brothers and sisters – and spouses – need forgiveness, so do parents.

From this we learned of Your boundless mercy and grace. You cared so much for mercy that You gave Your only begotten Son so that we may have mercy in the time of greatest need. And if You care so much for mercy and grace, You surely expect it of us toward others.

Father, we thank You for these things we learned in the family and for what we learned of You because of them.
Amen.

Frank L. Ford

FATHER OF MANKIND

There is a beautiful, meaningful prayer that we all pray together from time to time. It was written in 1872 by an American poet and set to music. It's in most hymnals now, over 140 years later. The song, or prayer, reflects the Quaker background of its author. It can't be read, or prayed, hurriedly. It must be contemplated as it is read or sung. The author is John Greenleaf Whittier. The song is "Dear Lord and Father of Mankind."

> DEAR LORD AND FATHER OF MANKIND,
> FORGIVE OUR FOOLISH WAYS,

We're foolish when we believe we're in control – when we walk alone, not even bothering to ask Your guidance. We're so foolish when we judge, forgetting that You are the Judge of all. And even more foolish when we judge harshly, forgetting the countless times we've been judged leniently – and forgiven. We're unbelievably foolish when we take for granted all that we have. We're saved! We're loved! We're needed! We even have material things in abundance for all our needs, all our wants, and even our whims! We have gadgets and luxuries so much we must buy space to store it all.

A Collection of Prayers

RECLOTHE US IN OUR RIGHTFUL MIND,

Your Word teaches us that we can be transformed by the renewing our mind so that we are not conformed to this world. Help us to shake off this stupor induced by self-centeredness. Show us the insanity of our self-righteousness.

IN PURER LIVES THY SERVICE FIND,

Father, Your Word and our experience teaches us that if we draw nigh to You, You will draw nigh to us. Without Your nearness, Your indwelling, we have no hope for purity for we know that in us dwells nothing good. Lord, we openly confess that if our lives are to be pure, it is because of Your purity – not our own for all our righteousness is as filthy rags. Let us remember that Your service is service to those – in our home, at work, and wherever we find others in need. Lord, we sense that if You had meant for us to do great things, You would have given us great powers, and since most of us do not have great powers, we must be meant to do small things – encouraging, sympathizing, helping with unpleasant tasks – footwashing type of work. But whether great or small, O Lord, let us find Your service and perform it with a cheerful heart.

Frank L. Ford

IN DEEPER REVERENCE, PRAISE!

Father, many words stir feelings of reverence for You in our hearts such as omnipotent, omniscient, omnipresent, eternal, the Only Begotten Son, justice, mercy, heaven. But these are only feelings and thoughts of reverence. Our prayer is that we will revere You so deeply that we will reverence You with our lives. So deeply that Your will becomes more important than our own. That Your will becomes our will and our very living becomes an act of praise.

DROP THEY STILL DEWS OF QUIETNESS, TILL ALL OUR STRIVINGS CEASE. TAKE FROM OUR SOULS THE STRAIN AND STRESS, AND LET OUR ORDERED LIVES CONFESS
THE BEAUTY OF THY PEACE.

In the name of Him who taught us to call You Father. Amen.

A Collection of Prayers

GO ASK

"Don't ask me to explain for you, how one can start again; How hardened hearts could soften like a child's.

Don't ask me how to reason out the mysteries of life, or how to face its problems with a smile.

Go ask the man who's found the way, through tangled roads back home to stay, when all communications were destroyed.

Go ask the child who's walking now, who once was crippled – then somehow, her useless legs were made to jump for joy.

Go ask the one whose burned-out mind has been restored. I think you'll find the questions not important as before.

Don't ask me if he's good or bad. I only know the guilt I had is gone, and I can't tell you anymore.

Don't ask me how to prove to you why I know God is there, and I know that He could care for you.

Don't ask me why someone so great would choose to walk with me and trade my broken life for one that's new.

Go ask the child who's got a Dad to love away the hurt he had before this man called Jesus touched their lives.

Go ask the one whose fears have fled, whose churning heart was quieted when someone whispered peace to all her strife.

Go ask the man to tell you more whose life was just a raging war inside himself until the Savior came.

I don't pretend to be so wise, I only know He touched my eyes and nothing else will ever be the same."

Lord, again we bring problems, pains, hurting, that we have no hope of resolving – except to go ask You. Experience has taught us that You are the One to whom we should go, and that nothing is too hard for You. As our children brought us whatever was broken because they believed we could fix it and brought us whatever hurt because they believed we could take away the hurt, we come to You because You have all power in heaven and earth – and because You care about us – because You love us.

Father, we bring our most precious possessions to You – our families, our friends, people who have touched our hearts. We bring You broken bodies, broken health, broken hearts, broken relationships, and broken lives. These we hold up to You, Father. We ask for full recovery, complete healing, mended hearts, and fully restored relationships. We ask for a second chance – a clean slate.

We do not ask for half-measures. We know You do not deal in half-measures. We ask You to bring all Your power to bear on these problems and needs. And we believe that when You do that, everything will be made right. We don't know how, or why, or when, but we believe it will. Help us to trust You as our children trust us. We ask all in His name. Amen.

A Collection of Prayers

GOD'S GRACE

John Newton, at 82, near death, almost blind, with fading memory said, "My memory is almost gone, but I remember two things – I'm a great sinner and Christ is a great savior."

"At the cross, at the cross, where I first saw the light and the burden of my heart rolled away! It was there, by faith, I received my sight . . ."

What actually happened, according to Paul, was because of His great love for us. God, who is rich in mercy, made us alive with Christ even when we were dead in transgressions. It is by grace we have been saved. Through faith – and this not from ourselves, it is the gift of God.

> Before I received my sight, I was without hope.
> Now I am full of hope!
> Before I received my sight, I was a slave of sin.
> Now I am free!
> Before I received my sight, I was bound for Hell.
> Now I am destined for Heaven!
> Before I received my sight,
> I was undeserving of God's grace and mercy!

Now I am still undeserving of God's grace and mercy, but I have it. I don't understand the mystery of grace – only that it meets us where we are, but does not leave us where it found us.

Father, only Your grace could make sinners like us as dear, as near as Your Son. Only grace could make the offer to everyone. Father, there are people so evil, so vile that we who are here now would not want to be in the same room with them, and justifiably so, but to them, You offer the living water.

You, the Almighty God who knows no sin, offer grace to people who have only known sin. And this is the very nature of Your grace. The worst of us is not treated as one who has escaped by the skin of his teeth nor as one put on probation until he is proven, but as sons and daughters. We are not relegated to entering Your kingdom through the back door with our head hung in shame. We are allowed to approach the throne boldly, as a member of the royal family. Only by grace could this happen.

When we've been trying to fathom Your grace for 10,000 years, we'll be no closer than when we'd first begun. Because of Your grace, when this flesh and heart shall fail, and mortal life shall cease, I shall possess, within the veil, a life of joy and peace.

In His name, Amen.

HEART

In speaking about the heart recently, the minister stated that we can't put everything in our heart, so we must decide what is important to put there. The heart will take what we give it, whether good, or bad, or valuable, or useless. Knowing this, we agree that we should choose good things.

I would like to look at another aspect: the order in which we put things into our heart – that's important, too. Let me illustrate.

Imagine a large container. We will fill the container with various sized things. Imagine too, the larger the item, the more valuable it is. We'll use softballs, pebbles and sand.

If we put sand in first, that's all we have room for. We'll have lots of it, but it's not worth much. So we begin with the largest – the softballs – vital things – God, prayer, humility, and fill it. And it's full.

That's our life – the vital things.

But we can add pebbles – important things – other people. The pebbles will fall through the spaces between the softballs until we've filled it – and it's full.

That's our life – the vital things and the important things.

We can still add sand – some things for us. The sand will fall through the spaces between the softballs and the pebbles until we've filled it, and it's full.

That's our life.

First, there are God things – then there are other things – and then our things.

Father, our heart's desire is to always seek first Your kingdom at every decision point, at every fork in the road.

Sometimes it's difficult. We lose sight of our aims. We allow ourselves to become distracted by things, by cares, by concerns, leaving what's important unattended to see to what's urgent – or what we call urgent – because that justifies our focus on what it pleases us to do.

Neither do we always follow our heart's desire. Sometimes we yield to the eye's desire, or to selfish desires, or to baser desires – and those things are added to us, cluttering our heart with stuff that neither edifies nor satisfies but takes space that might have been occupied by valuable things.

Help us think more critically about what we see and hear and do – things that will find their way into our heart.

Father, we always strive to make a good appearance, and doing so we please ourselves and each other. But You don't look at our appearance – You look at our heart. You see where our treasure is, and You know what we are.

A Collection of Prayers

Take away our heart of stone, Father. Give us a heart of flesh. Put Your Spirit in us and move us to follow Your desires and keep Your laws.

We pray in Jesus name, Amen.

Frank L. Ford

IN AWE

We walk into the service thinking we've been here, we've done this – ho-hum. We've grown accustomed to His grace. The best antidote I know for this disease is His second phrase of the Lord's Prayer: "Hallowed be Thy name."

The theme of Revelation Chapter 4 is the hallowing of God's name. John is caught up into heaven and finds himself in the midst of a worship service. Listen –

> "At once I was in the Spirit and there before me was a throne in heaven with someone sitting on it. And the one who sat there had the appearance of jasper and carnelian. A rainbow, resembling an emerald, encircled the throne. Surrounding the throne were twenty-four other thrones and seated on them were twenty-four elders. They were dressed in white and had crowns of gold on their heads.
>
> From the throne came flashes of lightning, rumblings and peals of thunder. Before the throne, seven lamps were blazing. These are the seven spirits of God. Also before the throne there was what looked like a sea of glass, clear as crystal.
>
> In the center, around the throne, were four living creatures. Day and night, they never stopped saying, "Holy, holy, holy is the Lord God Almighty, who was, and is, and is to come."

> Whenever the living creatures give glory, honor and thanks to Him who sits on the throne and who lives forever and ever, the twenty-four elders fall down before Him who sits on the throne and worship Him who lives forever and ever. They lay their crowns before the throne and say, "You are worthy, our Lord and God, to receive glory and honor and power, for You created all things, and by Your will they were created and have their being."

To hallow means to set aside as special or holy. It has to do with reverence, awe, and wonder. The prophet Isaiah said in the presence of God, "Woe is me. I am undone." When I came into the presence of God, I came apart – I unraveled before God. "I am undone." When John saw the glory of the risen Christ, he said, "I fell at His feet as though dead."

C.S. Lewis said, "A human in the presence of God is going to feel one of two ways. Either you feel like a small, dirty object or you lose thought of yourself altogether. The latter is by far, preferable."

"O, Lord, my God, when I in awesome wonder." Isn't that what's missing? Awe and wonder in the presence of God. With our lips and with our lives, you and I are to look up into the face of a holy, loving majestic God and say, "Hallowed be Thy name."

In the Bible, God is not simply holy – God is called holy, holy, holy. Holy to the third power. In Hebrews, emphasis comes through repetition. When Jesus wanted His hearers to pay close attention He would say, "Verily, I say to you." If He was saying something of ultimate importance, He said, "Verily, verily." God is holy, holy, holy.

Remember before whom you stand. The shattering wonder of our worship is that we come into the presence of a holy, majestic God, glorious and enthroned in radiance, with every angel's eye in heaven fixed on Him, and we call Him "Father" for He loves us with unfathomable love.

In the words from an old hymn,

> "The love of God is greater far that tongue or pen can ever tell,
> It goes beyond the highest star and reaches to the lowest hell,
> The guilty pair, bowed down with care, God gave His Son to win,
> His erring child He reconciled and pardoned from his sin.
>
> Could we with ink the ocean fill and were the skies of parchment made,
> Were every stalk on earth a quill and every man a scribe by trade,
> To write the love of God above would drain the ocean dry,
> Nor could the scroll contain the whole, though stretched from sky to sky."

This is the God before whom we stand. When we pray the Lord's Prayer we step into the presence of this God. A place we have no business being, but where instead of being annihilated or thrown out, you and I are welcomed, embraced, and received.

A Collection of Prayers

I want to tell you a story.

She ran away from home. She boarded a ship for America. When she arrived at Ellis Island, all the passengers were told they were to line up in two parallel lines with hundreds of people in each line. As she was standing there, an immigration official came by checking documents. She had none. The official had a block of chalk and put a white "X" in chalk on her arm, meaning she was to be deported immediately. She had no sponsor, no passport, no family and no status.

As soon as the immigration official left, a stranger in the other line reached out with his hand and brushed the white "X" off her arm. When they got to the head of the line he said, "She's with me." She lived the rest of her life in America married to him.

You and I were born into this world with an "X", without status and without hope before God. But there is One who comes to us, who reaches out His nail-pierced hand, and wipes that "X" of shame and guilt and says to us, "You're with Me."

Remember before whom you stand.

Father, thinking on these things, we are awakened from our stupor and our preoccupation with ourselves. We understand Isaiah when he said, "Woe is me for I am undone", and John when he fell at His feet as though dead.

When we bowed before You at the cross we said, "Nothing in my hands I bring." When we contemplate standing before the throne, we realize again that there is nothing in us that is worthy of offering to You. The awesome wonder is that we come into the presence of a holy God, glorious and enthroned in radiance and we may call Him Abba – Father!

Why would we not bow in humble adoration? Our Father who art in heaven, hallowed be Thy name for Thine is the kingdom, and the power, and the glory forever.

Amen.

A Collection of Prayers

INCARNATION

We know that one day the Word became flesh – that's what we call the Christmas story. The second person of the trinity – Jesus – became a created being – a man. I never fully realized until recently what an awesome thing God did that day.

Jesus had to become a man in order to reach men. And when God allowed Jesus to become man more than God, He ran the risk that Jesus would act more like a man than God. And since He had become a man – a weak man – like me, He could very well have acted like a weak man, like me.

Satan played to that possibility. He said, "You can turn the stone to bread; you can satisfy all your needs." He said, "He will command His angels concerning You. They will lift up their hands, so that You will not strike Your foot against a stone." He said, "You are immortal."

Atop a very high mountain, so He could see all the kingdoms of the world and their splendor, he said, "All this I will give You if You bow down and worship me." Satan offered this man – a man like me and you:

— Satisfaction of all his needs and wants
— Immortality
— Ultimate power in the world.

Could I resist? Would you? I want to believe that I would have refused the temptation, but I honestly doubt that I would.

Satan offered everything!

And if Jesus had truly become a man – and He truly had – He could have bolted. He could have become the master of the earth. Could it really have happened? I believe it could. Did God take a chance that it would happen? I believe He did.

Father, You teach us in Your word that if we are to follow Jesus we must deny ourselves and take up our cross. We see that Jesus did not ask anything of us that He was not willing to do. He denied Himself food after fasting forty days. He denied Himself all the kingdoms of the world. He would not deny Himself the cross. He humbled Himself and became obedient to death, even death on the cross.

Therefore God exalted Him to the highest place and gave Him the name that is above every name, that at the name of Jesus every knee should bow, in heaven and on earth, and under the earth, and every tongue confess that Jesus Christ is Lord, to the glory of God the father.

Father, let us fix our eyes on Jesus, the author and perfecter of our faith, who for the joy sat before Him endured the cross, scorning its shame, and sat down at the right hand of the throne of God.

In His name, Amen.

INDECISION

Life has a way of leading us to junctures – to bends in the road, to crossroads, to dead ends. Sometimes it happens as subtly as the changing of seasons. Sometimes it happens with the suddenness of an explosion. And when we realize what has happened we say, "Here I stand," with one foot on what was, one foot on what will be – whatever that is.

Always, the worst part is not so much where we find ourselves, but not knowing what the ultimate outcome will be. We look for meaning – why are we in this situation at this time? We look for direction – where do we go from here? The indecision – not knowing how to proceed tears at us like a buzz saw.

Father, in spite of all Your teachings about Abraham, about Job, about Joseph, about walking by faith when we find ourselves in adversity, we want to walk by sight. We want answers. We want to know how long before there is a solution. We want to know what the solution is. We want to know how the solution will be affected. We fret, and stew, and doubt. And when we are reminded that You have never failed us, though we have been in need like this before, we take heart – and then we fret, and stew, and doubt.

Father, in our selfish desire to know the why, and how, and when, we feel like the Psalmist when he said, "Why, O Lord, do You stand far off? Why do You hide Yourself in time of trouble?"

It seems that the more we cry out, the more You are silent, and the more You hide Yourself. Father, are we so proud, so hard of heart, that this is the way we must be taught to walk by faith?

But if we stop thinking of ourselves, and our desires, we realize that You were also silent with Job, and Abraham, and Joseph – and even with Jesus in the garden. Forgive us Lord for making our will more important to us than Your will.

Thank You for making us realize that, "Here we stand," not in trouble, not forsaken and alone. "Here we stand" – at Your throne seeking Your will for our life. "Here we stand" in complete confidence that You make all things work together for our good.

Help me to trust in You with all my heart and lean not on my own understanding.

Amen.

A Collection of Prayers

INDEPENDENCE

We therefore, the representatives of the United States of America in general congress assembled, appealing to the Supreme Judge of the world for the rectitude of our intentions do this in the name and authority of the good people of these colonies solemnly publish and declare that these United Colonies are and of right ought to be free and independent states. This declaration, as you know, was made on July 4, 1776. Great Britain, of course, did not agree and these United States were not free and independent that year, nor the next, nor the next.

In 1782, the British cabinet agreed to recognize this country's independence. The Treaty of Paris formalizing peace between Great Britain and the United States was signed in 1783 – over seven long years from declaration to ratification. We made a declaration of independence the day we turned to Jesus. We declared ourselves to be free and independent of Satan and self, and God has recognized that declaration – yet the war goes on. Peace is not yet. Please pray with me.

Father, we're thankful to have been born in a land where freedom is valued above all else. We praise You for valuing our freedom so highly that You gave us free will over our minds and bodies. We realize the perils that come with freedom. We know that freedom misunderstood or misused can result in much harm to ourselves and to others. But we know that Your Word offers promises of wisdom, chastening and correction to enable us to handle the freedom that we have.

We give thanks that our country's principles are indeed noble and good and worthy of pride. Our practices from time-to-time have been our shame. Please forgive us.

Our country realized its independence in seven years. In our lives it seems to come much slower. I've learned a lot, but I'm not much wiser. I've acquired a lot, but I haven't gained much. I've aged a lot, but I haven't grown much. Paul dealt with this. He said, "O wretched man that I am. Who will deliver me from this body of death?" And when he had given in to his frustration, when he felt that self would be the death of him, then he could hear Your answer, "Deliverance comes through Jesus Christ our Lord."

As our young country needed and received help from other countries in the fight for independence, the Spirit also helps our infirmities in our fight for independence for we know not how we should pray as we ought, but the Spirit itself makes intercession for the saints according to Your will.

All of our striving amounts to nothing. By Your grace we are saved; it is not of ourselves. It is Your gift. In everything, Father, we find Your grace sufficient. Because of that marvelous grace, however we feel, however dark things seem, we know it is well with our souls.

A Collection of Prayers

When peace like a river attendeth my way,
When sorrows like sea billows roll,
Whatever my lot, Thou has taught me to say,
It is well, it is well with my soul.
Though Satan should buffet, though trials should come,
Let this blessed assurance control,
That Christ has regarded my helpless estate,
And has shed His own blood for my soul.
My sin, not in part, but the whole,
Is nailed to the cross and I bear it no more.
Praise the Lord, praise the Lord, O my soul.
And Lord, haste the day when the faith shall be sight,
The clouds be rolled back as a scroll,
The trump shall resound, and the Lord shall descend,
Even so, it is well with my soul.

Father, hear our prayer in the name of Him who shed His own blood for our souls.

Amen.

Frank L. Ford

LIKE DAVID

Sing to the Lord a new song,
Sing to the Lord all the earth,
Sing to the Lord, praise His name,
Proclaim His salvation day after day.
Declare His glory among the nations,
His marvelous deeds among all peoples.
For great is the Lord and most worthy of praise.
Splendor and majesty are before Him.
Strength and glory are in His sanctuary.

Father, our prayer today is a prayer of praise for Your caring for us, for healing us, for lifting us, for giving us worth and sense of worth – for loving us. There are times when it seems that our dreams are dust and our plans are laid waste. Our intentions are of no consequence. When we're tempted to say, "What's the use?"

We feel like David when he said, "The waters have come up to my neck. I sink in the miry depths where there is no foothold. I have come into the deep waters. The floods engulf me. I am worn out calling for help. My throat is parched. My eyes fail, looking for God."

But experience has taught us that we should never, never, never, give up, because You never, never, never fail us. We never feel so badly that we can limit Your power to help us.

A Collection of Prayers

We're never so dejected that You can't cheer us – never so far away that You can't reach us – never so alone You can't find us. We're never so sick or so tired, or so sick and tired, of life that You can't bear us up on eagle's wings.

We pray like David when he said, "I pray to You, O Lord, in the times of Your favor. In Your great love, O God, answer me with Your sure salvation. Rescue me from the mire. Do not let me sink. Do not let the flood waters engulf me or the depths swallow me up or the pit close its mouth over me. Answer me, O Lord, out of the goodness of Your love."

Forgive our weakness, Father, for sinking into worry and discouragement. You've helped us so many times we should have learned once and for all not to give Satan a foothold. We should be able to say with Job, "Though He slay me, yet will I trust Him."

In You, we have found a cove, a shelter, a refuge, a hideout to run away to from the storms of life. At the same time, we find in You a tower, a fortress, and a high ground from which to launch an assault on the things of this world that would defeat us.

And in You, we find the strength to believe in ourselves. You've give us will, intelligence, and determination – the tools that we need to fight many of our own battles, but never alone, for You never forsake us.

We rejoice like David when he said, "I love the Lord, for He heard my voice. He heard my cry for mercy. Because He turned His ear to me, I will call on Him as long as I live. The Lord is gracious and righteous. Our God is full of compassion. The Lord protects the simple-hearted. When I was in great need, He saved me. Be at rest once more, O my soul, for the Lord has been good to you."

And finally, we praise like David when he said, "It is good to praise the Lord and make music to Your name, O Most High. To proclaim Your love in the morning and Your faithfulness at night. You make me glad by Your deeds, O Lord. I sing for joy at the works of Your hands."

This is our prayer, in Jesus name. Amen.

LISTENING

Father, I know that any changes in my daily life are, in the final analysis, up to me. I know equally well that You are able and willing to help me. You have helped me and will help me in anything that is good.

I resolve to be a better listener, to spend more time listening, and to listen more closely.

Father, when I listen to those who rejoice, let me rejoice with them. When I listen to those who sorrow, let me feel their sorrow. Help me to listen to the complainer, too, and to hear the needs that lie deeper than the complaint.

When I listen to those who need to express their feelings, those who need an ear, make me a good listener. When I hear those problems and needs, and out of my experience and imagined wisdom I have the answer, make me a very good listener.

Help us all to listen to the children especially. Of all their needs during their formative and maturing years, one of the greatest needs is to express the ideas and opinions they are forming. Help us to remember that every imperfect idea does not have to be corrected.

Help us all to listen to parents. They have a need to express concerns, frustrations, victories, and advice too, that require a listener. Parents alone can be counted on to love us more than all others, all of our life. And one of a parent's greatest joys is to be listened to – really listened to.

Help me to listen more closely to my friends and know them better. Help me to listen to the stranger and perhaps make a friend.

Father, there are times that I don't want to be a good listener. I need Your help with this. When gossipers speak, let me be deaf. When negative, defeating comments are made, let me be forgetful. When I hear insults, let me be forgiving. Guide me in when to turn a deaf ear.

Father, my greatest need and desire is to listen more closely, and more often, to You. Help me to be still and let You speak to my heart. Help me to be patient and wait for You. Remind me that I cannot listen faster than You speak.

Give me the courage to be totally, completely, honest with You when I ask You to listen. Sometimes I withhold from my prayers things that are difficult for me to talk or think about. I know that if I am not open and honest – if I don't empty my heart – I will not hear You speak.

Father, now while we're quiet and our hearts have been opened to You, let us remain quiet for a moment more to listen to the stillness of our own hearts – or perhaps we may hear Your voice. Amen.

A Collection of Prayers

LITTLE THINGS

Theology is defined as the study of God and His relation to the world. It seems to me to be rather a study of religion.

I believe that scientists are studying God by learning what He has done – regardless of how they think He did it.

Astronomers have plotted the heavens. They have learned the schedule that God put in place – the seasons, the appearance of constellations and comets – all of these can be predicted for years to come. They have plotted the path and the position of suns that dwarf our sun.

God did this and much more in the five days before He made Adam. He also made morning glories which live only a day but bloom in profusion. And in those five days He made the violets, and microbes and a vast world that is hidden under a microscope.

And all He did, He did in glorious color. Computer makers boast of a 256 color palette. You know we've seen that many shades of green on a spring day.

These things are awe-inspiring. And they are because they reveal God in his glory. This, I believe, is theology. This is studying God.

How He deals with you and with me is not religion; it's life – life as God reveals it to us in our Lord, Jesus.

I found a poem entitled, "A Businessman's Prayer," by William Ludlum. I'd like to read it. It's not on the same subject that I've been talking about, but captures the feeling better than I can.

"Dear Lord, I do not hesitate to thank Thee for things truly great; The universe is Thine and all accomplishment is at Thy call. Lord, of each mountain art Thou. Still art Thou of each little hill.

It pleases me to know I may receive Thy backing every day in all the larger things of life, however gigantic be the strife. But this thought pleases best of all – Lord art Thou of the very small.

No matter how great be my goal, 'tis little tasks make up the whole, and the sure knowledge that Thou art the Lord of each gives to my heart the strength to face them one by one until the larger task is done.

When 'tis completed, I agree the finished products due to Thee. I thank Thee for it as a whole, but deep down in my toiling soul, my gratitude the greater clings to Thee as Lord of little things."

Father, thank You for Your gift that is too wonderful for words. The whole earth is full of Your glory – Isaiah 6:3. All of nature is Your canvas. Let us stand still and consider Your wondrous works – Job 37:14.

Glorious, majestic are Your deeds; Your righteousness endures forever – Psalms 111.3.

Lord art Thou of the universe, and Lord art Thou of the very small.

You made us out of the dust of the earth, then by sheer love and grace and Jesus' blood, You gave us to believe – to know – that we are Yours forever!

Father, may our hearts sing our thanks through endless ages.

In Jesus' name. Amen.

Frank L. Ford

LOVING FATHER

I believe prayer is or may be more than just asking God for something. I believe prayer is or may be a dialog – two-way communication with God. It's in the broader sense that I'd like to lead the prayer today.

I believe God makes plans, ordains events, creates circumstances, raises up people, and does a hundred things to create blessings for His children – blessings that encourage, strengthen, edify, and sometimes, simply delight His children. That's what fathers do, and He is a better father than any of us.

I'd like to talk about three ladies, their work and their words, that God ordained years ago to bless us today. Each was given a physical limitation, but certainly no spiritual limitation.

Fanny Crosby lost her sight to an eye infection and bungled medical care at the age of six weeks. She wrote over 8,000 songs, nineteen that grace the hymnal in your pews. Her name appears in the hymnal more times than anyone else – who is not an editor. Her songs are among most people's favorites. For example, Blessed Assurance, Jesus Keep Me Near The Cross, Safe in the Arms of Jesus, and Rescue the Perishing.

When a visitor commented that is was too bad God had allowed her to become blind, she said, "If I had been given a choice at birth, I would have asked to be blind for when I get to heaven, the first face I see will be the One who died for me."

Charlotte Elliott was a portrait artist and writer but was afflicted with crippling fatigue from the age of thirty-three. She wrote about 150 songs, is generally regarded as one of the finest English hymn writers – not so well known in this country, except for one song – Just as I Am. She said, "His grace surrounds me and His voice continually bids me to be happy and holy in His service – just where I am."

Myra Brooks Welch was raised in a musical family. Her special love was playing the organ. She became a poet, known worldwide. Because of severe, crippling arthritis, she became confined to a wheelchair, typing by holding a pencil in each hand to strike the keys of the typewriter.

The Touch of the Master's Hand

T'was battered and scarred, and the auctioneer
Thought it scarcely worth his while
To waste much time on the old violin,
But held it up with a smile.

"What am I bidden, good folks," he cried,
"Who'll start the bidding for me?
A dollar, a dollar, then, two! Only two?
Two dollars, and who'll make it three?

Frank L. Ford

Three dollars, once; three dollars, twice;
Going for three . . . ," but no,
From the room, far back, a grey-haired man
Came forward and picked up the bow;

Then, wiping the dust from the old violin,
And tightening the loose strings,
He played a melody pure and sweet
As a caroling angel sings.

The music ceased, and the auctioneer,
With a voice that was quiet and low,
Said, "What am I bid for the old violin?"
And he held it up with the bow.
"A thousand dollars, and who'll make it two?
Two thousand! And who'll make it three?
Three thousand, once; three thousand, twice;
And going and gone," said he.

The people cheered, but some of them cried,
"We do not quite understand
What changed its worth?" Swift came the reply:
"The touch of a master's hand."

And many a man with life out of tune,
And battered and scarred with sin,
Is auctioned cheap to the thoughtless crowd,
Much like the old violin.

A Collection of Prayers

A mess of potage, a glass of wine,
   A game, and he travels on.
He is going once, and going twice,
   He's going, and almost gone.

But the Master comes and the foolish crowd
   Never can quite understand,
The worth of a soul and the change that's wrought
   By the touch of the Master's hand.

In His name, Amen.

Frank L. Ford

MERCY

In First Chronicles, we read that King David did a very dumb thing, and then he did a very smart thing.

Satan provoked David to take a census of Israel. God was displeased. God told David that he must choose his punishment. He said, "I offer three things, choose one of these."

- Three years of famine,
- Three months of disaster at the hands of your enemies, or
- Three days of the sword of the Lord, with an angel of God ravaging all the territory of Israel.

When you read the chapter, you notice that Satan does not appear after verse one. Satan incites, he tempts, he spreads evil, but he is never around when the piper is to be paid.

When I read the three choices put before David, I thought, "What a hopeless situation. If there was ever a no-win case, this is it."

But then, I am not a man after God's own heart as David was. He didn't see a no-win; he saw what we call a no-brainer. He didn't hesitate. He said, "Let me fall in the hands of the Lord – He is merciful. I don't want to fall into the hands man nor nature. Let me fall into the hands of the Lord – He is merciful."

Father, how thankful we are that however sinful we've been, however stupid we've been, however self-serving we've been, we still can turn to You and expect mercy, knowing full well that we've given up all right to expect mercy.

Even without David's example, our hearts would somehow know that our best option is to fall into the hands of the Lord, for great are Your mercies. And we know, too, that we would not have called to You had You not been calling to us.

We know beyond all doubt that the last thing we want is justice, that what we need above all is grace – great are Your mercies.

We seek that mercy to cover all our sins, our shortcomings, our failures, our omissions. And by Your grace to make of us what we never could be otherwise be – and wonder upon wonder, You'll do it in the twinkling of an eye.

We ask this in Jesus' name, even dare to ask boldly, because – great are Your mercies. Amen.

Frank L. Ford

MISTER GOD

Jesus said, "I stand at the door and knock. If anyone hears My voice and opens the door, I will come in and eat with him, and he with Me."

I recently read a book that many people have found to be a blessing. The book is titled, "Mister God, this is Anna." A true story.

Anna, aged six, lived in England just before WWII. Her understanding of and acceptance of God is overwhelming. To her, God was "Mister God".

About God standing and knocking, she said, "That's very funny, that is. It makes me very important don't it? Fancy Mister God taking second place!"

Fynn, Anna's friend and the author of the book, put it this way. Mister God, even while He is at the center of all things, He waits outside us and knocks to come in. It is we who open the door. Mister God doesn't break it down and come in – no, He knocks and waits.

Heavenly Father, King of all Kings, who took on the form of a servant, not just to be slain in order to redeem us, but to continue to bless us by healing us, by leading us, by lifting us, by sustaining us when we could never hold on and You promised to do this for all of our days.

You are the creator of all things. You spoke all worlds into being. You are the Alpha and Omega. And yet – and yet You stand at the door and knock. Fancy Mr. God taking second place – to such as I.

Father, after all You have done to make salvation possible to all, You make us an all-important part of the equation. You knock and wait for us, clothed in our filthy rags as it were, to open the door to the Lord of Lords and actually put into our hands the power to leave You standing.

And at the same time, You call us, plead with us, by Your Holy Spirit to open the door and invite You in – for our good – not Yours. Thank You for Your immeasurable love.

In Jesus' name, Amen.

Frank L. Ford

MOTHERS

It's interesting that the Bible presents God as a father, but He acts like a mother. When I think of God as a rock, or a fortress, or powerful, I think of my father. But when I think of God as patient, even longsuffering, when I think of God as faithful – loving me in spite of my actions, when I think of God being concerned about my soul – I think of my mother.

If it sounds like I'm trying to change the biblical image, I'm not. If it sounds like I'm saying that God is mother-like, I'm not. I'm saying exactly the opposite. Mothers, especially, are God-like.

I'm not too fond of some of our special days that seem to have been created by greeting card companies, but Mother's Day is one I would have voted for, given the opportunity. It's one that I can talk to God about.

Father, thank you for mothers! Thank You for what a woman becomes when she gives birth and raises a child. Thank You for what it means to the children of the world. We all give thanks for their years and years of molding and shaping while accepting a secondary role. Thank You for mothers who put their own desires into submission to satisfy ours – who would reduce themselves to being a spotlight to shine on us.

Thank You for that hot temper that scolded, and worse, to keep us from being what we would have been content to be.

Sometimes we're disappointed when we try to make them proud of us for some accomplishment, or recognition, and they don't seem to be quite pleased enough. But then, we realize that mothers are wiser than that. They're proud because of what we are – or will be.

I pray You will give all mothers patience, strength, and special help during those years when they only have hope. During the long time when they honestly wonder whether the child will ever learn what they're trying so hard to instill.

Father, we are all the beneficiaries of devoted mothers. Please don't let us commit the sin of just taking the benefits for ourselves. Let us think what good things have come to us through sacrifice and dedication and practice those things in our life. What a pity if all that hard work and patience should last only one generation. Help us to be like our mothers – not to our children only, but to all children, to our mates, to our friends. Let us keep alive the value of believing in someone – the priceless heritage of feeling good about ourselves.

Thank You, Father, for being so good to us. Thank You for mothers who act like You. Amen.

Frank L. Ford

OBLIGATIONS

Father, we ask Your help in the most far-reaching task we will ever undertake.

The things we do and say, and especially the things we are seen doing, may reach into future generations and may have a direct bearing on the souls of our children – and their children and others we'll never know.

Impress upon our hearts our obligations, but also teach us what our obligations are not. Solomon and Jesus teach us to train them – and to <u>let</u> them. It's often difficult not to impose the benefits of our wisdom and experience on them, but help us remember that, as the poet said, they have their own thoughts. They dwell in the house of tomorrow which we cannot visit.

Remind us to temper the urge to impose the fruits of our experience — for life goes not backwards nor tarries with yesterday.

Teach us to listen more and learn that we are not always required to share our wisdom.

Thank You for the joys that accompany this awesome task.

A Collection of Prayers

Father, it lifts our hearts to know that You want for our children the same things we do. And even though sometimes it seems that our dreams will not be realized, we can happily place our faith in You and find hope and encouragement.

Thank You for loving our children!

Today, with Your help, by Your strength and wisdom, we rededicate our children and ourselves to You.

Amen.

ONE

If you knew you had a day to live, what would you do? We're fond of posing this question in order to focus on what's important. Jesus faced this situation – He knew His time had come and a good deal of what He did has been kept for us.

He gave a new commandment: Love one another as I have loved you.
He gave us the Lord's Supper.
He taught the disciples the importance of serving.
He washed the disciples' feet.
He taught Peter the foolishness of boasting – even if for a noble intent.
He promised the Holy Spirit.
He explained the vine and the branches.
He gave warnings of persecution
He comforted the disciples.

And He prayed.

He prayed first for Himself – that He might be glorified – so He could glorify God. Then, He prayed for the disciples – for their protection and their sanctification, and then He prayed for all believers – that's us. Not for wealth, nor for health, and not for eminence, but that we would be one. This is what He prayed: "That all of them may be one, Father, just as You are in me and I am in You."

I read somewhere years ago that the greatest hindrance to effective Christianity is our refusal to believe that we are one.

Let's pray about it.

Father, You have taken away our sin, but because of our stubborn will, there is still too much of us in us. Our pride makes us want to be right even if – perhaps especially if – others are wrong. It makes us want to be special in being right, rather than being special because we have relinquished self and become a servant to all.

We confess that we have done very poorly in being one. We have chosen rather to be "the one."

Father, if we would yield self to the Savior and act as one, what a force we could be for good. If we would yield self to the Savior and pray as one, what a force we could be for God. Father, I believe it happened in the first century. I believe it could happen now – if we would yield our stubborn will.

Father, we confess that we have been taken in by the same lie that Adam and Eve were taken in by – the appeal to our ego – the god of self.

We pray that You have not and will not give up on us, and that we will not give up, but will still try with renewed effort to be one as You wished. We pray that we will do whatever it takes to walk together. Help us to learn that we need not decide right and wrong. We are not called to be judges – only to be faithful. Help us to be ready to concede, to yield, to make peace – to be one – to be obedient. In His name, Amen.

Frank L. Ford

OUTGROWING

One of the problems with growing up in church is that of outgrowing – or not outgrowing the things and the ways we were taught as a child.

One of those things we learned is that prayer is us asking God for things. To grow up with that same idea is to have missed the point.

We've learned that it's not just asking – talking is better. Then we learn that listening is better still. Then we learn that the real point is receiving. God gives Himself.

Father, we come to You as beggars, with no claims, no entitlements to what is Yours. But by Your grace, we may come as Your children, boldly approaching the throne, seeking not our will but Yours. Experience has taught us that we will leave with more than we thought to ask.

We thank You that in Your goodness and love, You care less about our wants than about our needs. You give peace, hope, strength, comfort, resolve and everything we need for the journey through this world.

And You teach us. We learn more of You with our head bowed and our eyes closed and our mouth shut than in anything else we do.

A Collection of Prayers

Father, beyond asking and receiving physical things, beyond asking and receiving spiritual things when we come to You, You give of Yourself. Help us to accept You.

Father, our great need is to learn of You.
It's to take You into ourselves.
We don't want to act like Jesus to become like Him –
We want to become like Jesus so we'll act like him.

You, above all else, are what we need.
You, above all else, are what we desire.
You, above all else, are the essential in our life.

Help us to yield and allow You to come into our hearts and fill us and we will be satisfied.

In Jesus' name. Amen.

Frank L. Ford

POOR IN SPIRIT

Jesus said, "Blessed are the poor in spirit."

It's interesting that what are probably the two best known and most revered passages in the Bible, the Ten Commandments and the Sermon on the Mount, do not offer us peace or comfort. They cannot make an honest or a thoughtful person feel good.

The commandments are unattainable. James said, "Whosoever shall kept the whole law and yet offend in one point, he is guilty of all." If anyone told us that they did all that Jesus said in the Sermon on the Mount, we would certainly think them so crazy or so shallow that they should be avoided.

Why would God, through the greatest of teachers, Moses and Jesus, give us teachings that are so far above our capacity that they can only lead to despair? These are God's standards and we should not, cannot argue with that, but why give them to us knowing that we can never hope to keep them?

I think the answer lies in the question. These commandments of God are meant to produce despair. Oswald Chambers said, "The bedrock of Jesus Christ's kingdom is poverty – not possession. When we realize we are incapable – that we haven't a hope – that spiritually we are bankrupt, Jesus says, "Blessed are you."

Why? Because only then are we trusting fully in His grace. St. Augustine said, "God gives where He finds empty hands." C.S. Lewis in Pilgrim's progress, refers to the Valley of Wisdom. He said it was known in earlier days as the Valley of Humiliation.

Father, we thank You that Jesus did not come to teach only. That He came to make us what He teaches we should be. We thank You for teachings that lead us to Jesus. We thank You more for Jesus, to whom the teachings lead us, for He did not say that His teachings are the way, the truth and the life, but He said, "I am the way, the truth and the life." He did not say come unto the words I teach, He said, "Come unto Me."

His commandments can only condemn us. We are too willful and too weak to obey. But He can save us. His strength is made perfect in our weakness.

Thank you, Lord, for teaching us to be poor in spirit, and thank You for the blessings that come to us when we are. Amen.

Frank L. Ford

PRAYER

When we pray, we usually have something to pray for or about. Prayer, we know is a vehicle; a means to an end. It's the means of asking God for our needs and desires. It's the means of praising Him because we're happy with our condition. It's a means for many things. Prayer is also an end in itself. Sometimes, we find ourselves, as the old spiritual says, "Standing in the need of prayer." Not in need of things or help – just in need of prayer. Let this prayer be not a means to an end, but an end.

Let me share with you what Annie Johnson Flint wrote in a poem entitled, "The Place of Prayer."

>The place of prayer is a humble place,
>and ere we enter there
>We must leave outside our garb of pride,
>and our load of worldly care.

>The place of prayer is a quiet place,
>and at the outer gate,
>The voice of our will we must firmly still,
>and bid our wishes wait.

A Collection of Prayers

The place of prayer is a holy place,
and ere we step therein
With unshod feet our God to meet,
we must put away our sin.

But the place of prayer is high enough
to bring Heaven's glory nigh,
And our need speaks clear to our Father's ear,
and is open to His eye.

And the place of prayer is wide enough
for Christ to enter there,
And the humble heart need not depart,
without that vision fare.

And the place of prayer is large enough
to hold God's riches stored,
And faith is the key of the treasury,
that opens the secret hoard.

Thank You, Father, for the experience of prayer. Thank You for the place of prayer and the wonder of it – that we can really move into a spiritual world and commune in a spiritual way with You, the almighty, all-knowing, and all-powerful God. And to do that we don't have to lose consciousness or obtain some state of ecstasy – we only need to bring our will into Yours. And while we remain in full control of our mind and body, our spirit, one with Yours, soars. We are at peace and have a sense of calm that we only experience with You.

Father, we know the world is too much with us. We are too busy with getting and having and with being busy. We have a thousand diversions. When we visit with You, there is nothing to bring, nothing to boast, nothing to hide, nothing to fear.

We know we are too occupied with sound. It seems there must be sound. If not talking, then radio, TV, recordings. Silence is so rare. It's become difficult for our society to handle it.

Thank You, Father, for this time. Thank You for hearing us. We see the wisdom of Your urging us to be still and know that You are God. Help us to live by that wisdom. Amen.

A Collection of Prayers

PRAYER OF PRAISE

I believe the best prayers are prayers of praise. To close the service, I would like to read part of the prayer of praise that King David offered when the Israelites gathered to give for the building of the temple some 3,000 years ago.

Praise be to You, O Lord, God of our father Israel, from everlasting to everlasting.

> Yours, O Lord, is the greatness
> And the power,
> And the Glory,
> And the majesty,
> And the splendor,
> For everything in heaven and earth is Yours.
> Yours, O Lord, is the kingdom;
> You are exalted as head over all.
> Wealth and honor come from You;
> You are the ruler of all things.
> In Your hands are strength and power to exalt and give strength to all.

Now, our God, we give You thanks and praise Your glorious name. Amen.

Frank L. Ford

PROMISES

Annie Johnson Flint, a favorite poet of many, including me, writes eloquently about God's promises – what He has promised and what He has not.

> God hath not promised skies always blue,
> Flower-strewn pathways all our lives through.
> God hath not promised sun without rain,
> Joy without sorrow, peace without pain.

Father, You have blessed us richly in many ways, and we thank You and praise You for that. For me, and for most of us, our life is so good that we sometimes think of it as a right. We think and feel that it should be sunny seven days a week and rain only at night. We think that being happy and at peace are, and should be, our natural state. We become greatly concerned and, quickly, when people or circumstances upset our apple carts, and wonder what went wrong – and our first words too often are, "Why me?"

Father, You have taught us by Your word, and by our lives and by all we experience, that a life free of care is not our natural state; that people coming together have always created friction and that we ourselves contribute to our frustrations.

Help us to look beyond our problems and be more concerned with how we deal with people and circumstances in Your sight than we are with the problems themselves. Give us grace to act in a way that is becoming to a child of God.

Father, the times of greatest frustration are those when we feel inadequate – when we know that we are caught up in a situation beyond our control, beyond our experience and beyond our capabilities – when we don't even know how to pray. And even then, You are our help.

Do Thou for me, O God! Helpless, I appeal to Thee.
What is best, I cannot tell. What is right, I cannot see. Blind, I dread to stand or go, and I fear to lose the way. For I know not what to do, and I know not how to pray. Hear my cry – do Thou for me; I can trust it all with Thee.

Thank You, Father, for the sure knowledge that –
    When our hearts are heavy, You offer comfort.
    When our hearts are troubled, You offer peace.
    When our hearts are empty, You offer love.
    When our hearts are void, You offer Your Son.

But God hath promised strength for the day,
    Rest for the labor, light for the way,
    Grace for the trials, help from above,
    Unfailing sympathy, undying love.

In the name of Christ Jesus in whom is the promise of life.

Frank L. Ford

PSALM 23

Father, when I feel lost and alone, I remember that,
> The Lord is my shepherd.

And when I think of how I wish for what is not, I'm reminded that,
> I shall not want.

When I am in turmoil and there is no peace,
> You make me lie down in green pastures.

When the storm waves of life are about to drown me,
> You lead me beside still waters.

When I am utterly dejected and discouraged,
> You restore my soul.

And when I feel as though I have no value, no purpose,
> You lead me in paths of righteousness for Your name's sake.

When I doubt that You care for me in a personal way, I remember that,
> Though I walked through the valley of the shadow of death, I feared no evil, for You were with me. Your rod and Your staff comforted me.

A Collection of Prayers

When I think I have no worth in Your sight,
> You prepare a table before me in the presence of my enemies. You anoint my head with oil; my cup runs over.

It is such a joy, and relief, and comfort – a blessedness – to know beyond doubt that whatever my lot in days to come,
> Surely goodness and mercy shall follow me all the days of my life. I will dwell in the house of the Lord forever.

Amen.

Frank L. Ford

RESURRECTION

Not surprisingly, I'm thinking about Jesus' resurrection today as many of you are. Each of the gospels records the resurrection of Jesus, but the resurrection of Lazarus as related in John 11 is where Jesus taught about resurrection. That is what I would like to pray about.

Jesus and His disciples heard that Lazarus, the brother of Martha and Mary, was ill in Bethany, but they didn't go there right away. By the time they did go, Lazarus had been dead four days. Martha heard that Jesus was coming and went out to meet Him. This is most of the recorded conversation between Jesus and Martha:

> Jesus said, "Your brother will rise again."
>
> Martha said, "I know he will rise again in the resurrection at the last day."
>
> Jesus said, "I am the resurrection and the life. He who believes in me will live, even though he dies; and whoever lives and believes in Me will never die. Do you believe this?"
>
> Martha said, "Yes, Lord, I believe that You are the Christ, the son of God, who has come into the world."

Father, as we read the account of Jesus and Martha's conversation, it seems that Martha envisioned a distant thing. She said, "He will rise." Even a far distant thing – she said, "He will rise at the last day."

But Jesus spoke a *now* thing. He said, "I *am* the resurrection and the life."

Father, I believe You have recorded this so that we do not have to live in fear of failing. So that instead, our joy may be full; so that we may have life more abundantly in the sure knowledge that we are safe in the arms of Jesus – we have a blessed assurance.

We thank You. We praise You for Jesus' resurrection because, as surely as He arose, we shall rise. As the poet said, "Dust thou art, to dust returnest, was not spoken of the soul." As we are a soul – a living, resurrected soul from the day Jesus came into our heart.

Thank You for this record of what Jesus taught about resurrection. That we live even though we die – a spiritual truth, not cast before swine nor readily understood by unbelievers, but bound up in the hearts of believers whose hearts have been purged of sins and in whom the Holy Spirit dwells.

We thank You that in this record Jesus said, "Did I not tell you that if you believed you would see the glory of God."

Frank L. Ford

And we believe that without reservation because we believe Jesus without reservation and look forward to the day when we too will see the glory of God because –

> Living, He loves us,
> Dying, He saved us,
> Buried, He carried our sins far away,
> Rising, He justified, freely forever,
> One day He's coming,
> Oh, glorious day!

In His name we pray. Amen.

SEPARATIONS

Father, hear the prayer we speak today – and those that we don't, or can't, put into words. Take these imperfect words and thoughts and medications and do with them as Your will.

Our thoughts have settled on the idea of separations. Our life begins with a separation from the womb; it ends with separation from this world. Our whole life in between is a series of separations which often leave us sad and sometimes bewildered.

At a very early age we were separated from the insulation of home and family and thrust into the world of formal education. Then we were separated from that world into the world of making a living. Many of us relocated and separated from old friends and familiar surroundings into a world of strangers.

By our own choice, we marry and separate ourselves from our families and assume responsibility for the lives of others. By maturing and learning, we separate ourselves from our childish ways into a world of seriousness and responsibility.

Help us to remember these things when we have difficulty dealing with people. Help us to remember that they may be experiencing a separation that we're not aware of; help us to be less critical and more forbearing.

We realize, Father, when we reflect, that separations, though they are often painful and leave us feeling empty, are part of

Your wisdom in designing our life in this world. We realize that separations are not just sad endings – they are really beginnings. The various stages of our life must end before the next can begin. There must be separations.

We see the wisdom of Your admonition in both the testaments to be separate – to come out of the world. Not until we let go of a worldly point of view are we ready to receive the good things You have to offer.

And even death, which we in our limited knowledge and understanding view as the final separation, is in fact the very thing that allows us to finally receive what You have held in store for us all our life. Only then can we experience that which Isaiah referred to when he said, "Since the beginning of the world, eye hath not seen, nor ear heard, neither have entered into the heart of man the things which God hath prepared for them that love Him."

So, Father, we thank You for the order of things that You so wisely have established. Thank You for the separations that are forced on us so that we can move on, and grow, and learn, and become what we are to be.

And thank You that the order of things You so wisely have established must include some things that never change – some areas where there is never a separation.

"For I am persuaded that neither death, nor life, nor angels, nor principalities, nor powers, nor things present nor things to come, nor heights, nor depths, nor any other creature shall be able to separate us from the love of God which is in Christ Jesus our Lord."

In His name, Amen.

Frank L. Ford

SERENITY

God grant me the serenity
To accept the things I cannot change,
Courage to change the things I can,
And wisdom to know the difference.
Living one day at a time,
Enjoying one moment at a time,
Accepting hardship as the pathway to peace.
Taking, as He did,
This sinful world as it is,
Not as I would have it.
Trusting that He will make all things right,
If I surrender to His will.
That I may be reasonably happy in this life,
And supremely happy with Him forever in the next.

May our Lord Jesus Christ Himself and God our Father, who loved us, and by His grace gave us eternal encouragement and good hope, encourage your hearts and strengthen you in every good deed and word.

Amen.

SERMONS

There is a story I've heard from multiple sources. I'm sure many of you have, too. I don't know whether it's true. It could be, but it's the kind of story that is sometimes made up to make a point, or to illustrate something that is true. In any case, I believe it's worth repeating.

In a very large church just as the Sunday morning service was getting under way, a not very clean and not at all neat young man came in, looked around for a seat, found none, sat down cross-legged in the aisle at the end of one of the pews toward the front.

Heads turned and came together as people buzzed about this person who obviously was not "one of them." Most of the buzzing was along the lines of "What will they do about this?"

After a while an old fellow with a cane slowly came down the aisle toward the young man. Now things really started buzzing. Will he ask him to leave? Will he find a way to show him this is not his crowd? What will the young man do? Will he react? Will he make a scene?

As the old man approached the young man, he stopped beside him, laid his cane down, and sat down cross-legged beside him. They turned to each other and nodded, "Hello." The service went on as usual.

After the service, the minister addressed the congregation and said, "You won't remember what you heard here this morning, but you will never forget what you saw."

Father, help us to remember that the loudest sermons are spoken in our actions, not in our words. We need not seek an opportunity to do great deeds, when there are many small deeds in such great need of being done.

Help us to quietly do them. May the God of hope fill you with joy and peace in your faith, that by the power of the Holy Spirit, your whole life and outlook may be radiant with hope.

We pray in Jesus' name, Amen.

THANKS

Luke tells the story of Jesus healing ten lepers. He didn't heal them immediately; He told them to go show themselves to the priests. As they went, they were cleansed. One of them, when he saw that he was healed, turned back, glorified God, fell on his face at Jesus' feet and gave thanks.

Jesus, Luke reveals, was disappointed that nine of the ten healed did not return to thank Him. If wisdom or common sense were not enough to cause them, or us, to know the value of giving thanks, there is the law, and the prophets, and history. In Leviticus, God gave instructions for Thank Offerings. When the Ark of the Covenant was returned to Israel, King David made the Levites responsible for burnt offerings and some were designated by name to give thanks to the Lord. To those Jews who were healed, and to Jesus, thanking God was as natural as breathing.

It's hard to imagine being healed and not giving thanks for it. It's not so hard to imagine my failing to give thanks for blessings that I take for granted and don't think to mention when I pray.

In a prayer of thanksgiving, we often name the things we're most thankful for; those things that have a great impact on our lives. Let us allow our thoughts to turn in another direction; not what we're least thankful for but what, perhaps, we least give thanks for – the little things.

Thank You, Father, for the little things that seem so much a part of living that we forget how blessed we are to have them.

Thank You for remembering:
- For remembering loved ones, now gone, and fond childhood memories.
- For bad times that are only a memory.
- For remembering our stupidity; it makes us more forgiving.
- For remembering our immaturity; it makes us more tolerant.
- For remembering our failures; it makes us more humble.

Thank You for hands:
- For big hands that brushed away our tears.
- For big hands that paddled us, out of love.
- For little hands held in ours, making us feel very good, and important, and very humble.
- For firm hands that clasp ours in a handshake that says loudly, but silently, "You're my friend."
- For gentle hands laid on our arm that say more than words could.

Thank You:
- For a sense of humor.
- For a sense of accomplishment.
- For a sense of well being.

A Collection of Prayers

Thank You for gifts, and cards, and invitations, and calls from those who care for us.

Thank You for old friends — and new ones.

Father, we realize that the little things that come our way are not things that just happen. They were sent our way by a King and loving Father who must delight in making His children happy.

Now, therefore, our God, we thank Thee and praise Thy glorious name.

Amen.

Frank L. Ford

THE CROSS

The cross has meant many things since it began to be used for crucifixions.

It has been and is now a favorite shape for jewelry because of its simplicity and elegance.

To Rome, it was the ultimate symbol of power because it wielded the power of life and death. It was the ultimate symbol of control. What could be more controlling than to be literally nailed to it?

To the victims, it was the ultimate judgment from which there could be no escape and no appeal.

To the Jews, it was a stumbling block.

To Christians, it is life – abundant life; it is salvation, it is mercy, it is grace, it is victory, it is a gift, it is sweet.

To Jesus, it was duty – doing what needed to be done, doing what must be done. It was sacrifice. He became our ransom – the sacrificial lamb slain in our stead.

In spite of what Rome and Satan intended for the cross to mean, Jesus was not ashamed. He was not defeated. He did not despair. He was not doomed. He is not dead.

He took away all the power and authority of Rome by yielding. In that act of love, He changed all that the cross had stood for and made it forever after stand for love, sacrifice, obedience and submission to the Father, and especially a symbol of love – "greater love hath no man." What had been a symbol of evil and death, Jesus made a symbol of love and life and hope.

Father, we stand amazed in the presence of Jesus the Nazarene and wonder how He could love us, sinners, condemned and unclean. We praise You for Your transforming power. We were blind, but now we see; we were lost, but now we're found.

It once seemed strange to us to sing wistfully about the "old rugged cross" – a symbol of death. But because we worship the one who hung on that cross, we sing of what it means to us.

We are thankful that Jesus on that cross transforms how we see everything. We are especially thankful for how we are seen by You because of Jesus on that cross.

It means that all barriers have been removed.

There is neither Jew nor Greek.
There is neither bond nor free.
There is neither male nor female.
We are one in Christ Jesus, thus we are Abraham's seed and heirs according to the promise.

Thank you, Father, for the power of the cross – the power of salvation. Amen.

Frank L. Ford

THE DASH IN BETWEEN

The more hurried our life gets, the more valuable is a walk through a cemetery. It's great for putting many things in perspective. No one there hurries anymore. Whatever was left undone remains undone and still the world goes on. It causes a person to think of their own epitaph and, although it's carved in stone after death, it is written while we live.

Some of the stones have lengthy verses, some a brief statement, some a phrase, and some nothing at all. The one thing they all have in common is that they document the entry into and the passing out of this life.

Some have the words, "Born" and the date, and "Died" and the date. Some have the dates with just a dash in between. One of the wisest persons I know remarked that the years aren't really important – the dash in between those years is everything. It is that dash through life – what we do and how we do it – that gives our brief life whatever meaning it has. That mad dash is the subject of my prayer.

Father, as we dash from place to place, trying to keep pace with our schedules; as we dash from one station in life to another, it's easy to forget where we're dashing – or why we're dashing – or even whether we should be dashing at all. Even in our service to You we often dash ahead, so caught up in the dash itself that we forget we're supposed to be following.

A Collection of Prayers

We're odd creatures. Sometimes we're concerned with doing great things so intensely that we forget that it's the little things that matter most – a smile, a kind word, patience with someone who moves or speaks more slowly than we'd like. Sometimes we become so preoccupied with trivia and with how things ought to be done that we can't see the forest for the trees. Jesus told the Pharisees they should have practiced justice, mercy and faithfulness without neglecting the tithing of the spices they owned.

Father, when we think of the cemetery, we remember that You are not the god of the dead, but are the God of the living, and we rejoice that those who've gone before us, who placed their trust in You are alive!

We share in that blessed hope – in Jesus, we will never die – we shall surely live! As we dash from one activity to another, from one station in life to another, help us to think of what we're doing – and why – and how. And help us to redeem the time by yielding every part of our life to You – for we are not our own - we have been bought – at a great price.

Father, when we think about that last year of this life, there are no words to adequately express our gratitude and joy in knowing that when the mad dash of this life is over, there will be a new way to record our days. There is a year of beginning for our entrance into Your kingdom, but there is no last year of eternal life – and there can be no dash in between.

When we've been there ten thousand years, bright, shining as the sun, we've no less days to sing God's praise than when we've first begun.

In the name of Him who is the resurrection and the life, we pray.

Amen.

THE FUTURE

Soon, we'll see the resumption of reenactments of Civil War battles. We won't see anyone or any group acting out the next war. It hasn't happened yet. We only know the past, though we seldom understand it. We struggle with the present. We know nothing of the future.

This is one of the many and vast differences between us and God. We can only know the past and can't cause a single thing to happen. God knows all that was, all that is, and all that will be.

For years I've wondered why Jesus said, "Take up your cross," before He had taken up His own cross. I wondered what those who heard it thought He meant. We understand what He said only in light of what He did. But when He said it, He hadn't done it.

That question was answered while I was studying the Passover in Exodus. God gave specific instructions for how the Passover would be remembered before it happened. That Passover in Exodus foretold the real Passover in Luke 22 where Jesus gave specific instructions for how the Lord's Supper would be remembered – before it happened.

The point is, we don't reenact nor do we celebrate what will happen simply because we don't know what will happen; we don't know the future.

God doesn't know the future – *He determines the future!*

Jesus said, "Take up your cross," not because it had significance in the past, but would have tremendous significance in the future.

Father, well did You say through Isaiah, "As the heavens are higher than the earth, so are My ways higher than your ways and My thoughts than your thoughts".

Sometimes, far too infrequently, we remove the blinders of pride and see You as You are, and see ourselves as we are, and we are humbled and ashamed. And when we think of how high You are, that You have all power in Heaven and earth, and can forgive our sins, and heal our diseases, and see that You are merciful and gracious, slow to anger and plenteous in mercy, we are glad. We should be glad because as far as the east is from the west, so far have You removed our sins from us.

Our days are as grass, but the mercy of the Lord is from everlasting to everlasting. Father, help us to take up Your cross and practice the compassion, the caring, and the love You practiced. Help us to take up our cross of obedience. Amen

A Collection of Prayers

THE LORD'S PRAYER

Most of us know the Lord's Prayer so well we can recite it easily – without thinking. That's my experience, but I find it more difficult to pray if I do think.

Jesus said, "After this manner, pray."

Our Father which art in Heaven –
Thank You for hearing us from heaven. We realize when we stop to think that although we know some things about Heaven, we don't really know where it is or what it is. We do know that You, the all powerful, all wise and all knowing God and Creator of all that is, or ever was, or ever will be, that You are there. We are amazed that our prayers about our concerns can reach You there simply addressed as "Our Father."

Hallowed be Thy name –
Your very name deserves to be hallowed. We don't hallow Your name by calling it in time of need and forgetting it until need strikes again. For this we ask Your forgiveness. Let us remember that Your name represents all that You are, and we must treat that name accordingly.

Thy kingdom come,
Thy will be done on earth as it is in Heaven –
May Thy kingdom come in all of its fullness, but may it not depend on me. I have so many things I feel I must attend to. I must earn a living, and I must spend time with my family and

friends, and I need time for recreation. Father, in truth, we want all these things and we want Your kingdom to come too. Help us to get our priorities straight.

Give us this day our daily bread –
Father, we are so accustomed to having our daily bread, and meat, and vegetables, and dessert, that it's easy to take it for granted. Thank You for our daily feast. We resolve to do more for the many, many men, women and children who don't have bread every day.

And forgive us our trespasses, as we forgive those who trespass against us –
Father, this is scary. This is hard to pray. In having us say this, Jesus is telling us that You're not going to treat us any better than we treat those people who offend us. He's telling us that if we harbor resentment for being ill-treated, You will hold that resentment against us. Please help us to deal with the resentment and the reluctance to forgive that is in our heart and, by Your grace, replace it with love. But thank You for the rest of the truth – that as we forgive, we may count on Your forgiveness. Weak as we are, we need Your forgiveness!

Lead us not into temptation, but deliver us from evil –
There is never a fear that we'll be lead into temptation when we do Your will, but there is always the lure of self-righteousness. Deliver us from the evil that so easily and so often we succumb to when we try to serve two masters.

For Thine is the kingdom, and the power, and the glory forever –
This moment, and all day, and tomorrow, and all week. When we're not in church – when temptations come, and when worry sets in, when frustrations rise, when loved ones are sick, or have left us, "Thine is the kingdom, the power and the glory forever."

Amen

Frank L. Ford

THE PRINCE OF PEACE

For unto us a child is born; unto us a son is given and the government shall be upon His shoulder and His name shall be called Wonderful, Counselor, The Mighty God, The Everlasting Father, and The Prince of Peace.

Mankind's only hope of attaining a right relationship with God was to somehow find a common plane, a way of relating to God. To somehow get to know God.

Man tried to get on God's level and failed miserably. In the Garden of Eden, Satan said, "In a day you eat of the forbidden fruit, your eyes will be opened. You shall be as gods." The woman saw that it was a tree to be desired to make one wise. The result was catastrophic.

Later, man said, "Let us build us a city and a tower whose top may reach unto heaven." The result was havoc.

We could never, in a million years, or in a million, million years, become as God. So God became – not as a man, but became man. John says, "In the beginning was the word, and the word was with God and the word was God." And, "The word was made flesh and dwelt among us." God became a baby! And when He did, He "raised us up together and made us sit together in heavenly places in Christ Jesus." Because of Him, we can know God!

A Collection of Prayers

On this day, in our society, we celebrate the fact that God became man; a miracle of unimaginable proportion, never performed before or since. He did it because He loved us. Thank You, Father, for doing for us what we could never do. Thank You for coming down, as one of us, and raising us up.

When Isaiah foretold Him, he said, "He was wounded for our transgressions, He was bruised for our iniquities. The chastisement of our peace was upon Him and with His stripes we are healed." And if He will see us pure, we must see Him wounded and bruised. If He will see us healed, we must see His stripes.

We thank You, Father, that we live in a nation that recognizes the birth of our Lord as a national holiday. And though some would like to do away with it, help us to remember that He came for them too and, but for Your grace, we would be as they are.

Father, we are like little children. The tinsel and bright lights sometimes blind us to the truth that underlies them. Let the lights be a reminder to us that, "The people that walked in darkness have seen a great light; they that dwell in the land of the shadow of death, upon them has the light shined."

Thank You for the baby Jesus who became the man Jesus. Thank You, "That the grace of God that brings salvation has appeared to all men, teaching us that, denying ungodliness and worldly lusts, we should live soberly, righteously, and godly, in this present world; looking for that blessed hope and the glorious appearing of the great God and our Savior, Jesus Christ."

We pray in the name of Him to whom every knee shall bow – The Mighty God, The Everlasting Father, and The Prince of Peace.

Amen.

THE ROBBER

Matthew Henry was an English clergyman who wrote a commentary of the Old and New Testaments and other material in the early 1700's. Once, on a trip to London, he was mugged. Afterward, he wrote this in his diary:

"Let me be thankful, first because I was never robbed before.

Second, although they took my purse, they did not take my life.

Third, because though they took all, it was not much.

Fourth, because it was I who was robbed, not I who robbed."

I can imagine that he also read, or recalled a passage from First Thessalonians, "Be joyful always. Pray continually. Give thanks in all circumstances. This is God's will for you in Christ Jesus."

Our loving Father, You are so good to us. We pause to give thanks. To praise You for Your patience with us, for forgiving us, for answering prayer, for hearing and speaking to us.

Amen.

Frank L. Ford

THE UGLY TREE

There is an old pine tree standing on a windblown hillside. This is no stately oak, nor a well-shaped maple. It's not even a tall, straight pine. It is one of the worst-looking trees I've seen. It's an ugly tree. Its trunk is curved, not once but twice – it looks like the letter "S". It has nubs where branches were and looks as if they've been torn off by the wind. Its lower part is covered with vines, giving it a grubby appearance like a three-day beard.

At the very top, there are a few green branches bearing cones. These branches don't reach upward – they seem to be groping outwardly. It is not a tree that anyone will rally to save if it lives for hundreds of years. This tree has taken the worst that nature could deal out, short of total destruction, and still stands. No one cares that it stands, but it stands.

Strangely, when I see this tree against a background of a clear blue sky on a sunny day, it has a majestic appearance. That majesty comes, not from its beauty, but from its sheer determination to stand and bear its fruit as best it can with so few branches.

Father, thank You for creating a world of beauty around us – for trees that give shade, and bear fruit, and provide lumber, and oxygen, and hold the soil together, and are beautiful to look at.

Thank You, especially, that even though You created beauty in everything You created, You did not make that beauty the most important feature of Your creations. Thank You for putting into Your creations a will to survive and to fulfill their purpose in spite of ugliness, wounds, abuse and handicaps.

Thank You for the lesson of the ugly tree. Some days I feel like that tree – ugly, scarred and alone. But I know You have instilled in me something of that tree's nature. I know that if I needed to be beautiful, I would be. If I am scarred, both the wounds and the healing are for my own good, somehow. If I feel alone, that draws me closer to You.

Thank You, Father, for seeing the inside of me, for teaching me that "Your beauty should not come from outward adornment, such as braided hair and the wearing of gold jewelry and fine clothes. Instead, it should be that of your inner self, the unfading beauty of a gentle and quiet spirit, which is of great worth in God's sight."

Let me draw inspiration from the ugly tree that You created. Help me to try harder to see inside of others, and myself, rather than this very temporary shell we live in.

Thank You that "Our citizenship is in heaven, and we eagerly await a Savior from there, the Lord Jesus Christ, who by the power that enables Him to bring everything under His control, will transform our lowly bodies so that they will be like His glorious body."

Frank L. Ford

THOU SHALT NOT

There are some who see Old Testament law as oppressive – a compendium of "thou shalt nots." To those people, I suggest a review of the following "thou shalt nots."

"Thou shalt not" vex a stranger nor oppress him.
"Thou shall not" afflict any widow, or fatherless child.
When you reap the harvest of your land, "thou shalt not" wholly reap the corners of thy field, neither shalt thou gather the gleanings of thy harvest. You shall leave them for the poor and the stranger. When thou cuttest down thine harvest in the field, and have forgotten a sheaf in the field, "thou shalt not" go again to fetch it: it shall be for the stranger, for the fatherless, and for the widow. The same commands applied for the harvest of the vineyards and the olive trees.

Not long ago, I was in conversation with some others and we agreed, as I imagine most of you will, that we are very richly blessed, and I wondered why we should be so richly blessed. These scriptures caused me to think that perhaps these rich blessings are not for me. Like the Israelite farmer's rich blessings, some of it is not for us – it is for others.

Father, Your commands that we are to live by show us what kind of God You are. You care for – indeed, You *love* – those who are not cared for. And You love us, Your children, so much You want us to love as You do, and You teach us how to do it. So did Jesus when He said, "As you did it to one of the least of these, you did it to Me."

Countless songs and poems have been written, and countless sermons have been preached, trying to capture how great You are, how great Your love is, and how much You care for all of Your children. Meaningful as these things are, beautiful as these things are, they are overshadowed by the fact that You've made it part of the farmer's way of life *not* to reap everything – because some of it You have provided for others – because You are a loving God and You have ordained it – by commandment.

Father, the more we understand Your love, the more we realize we do not really understand the depths of Your love. You grow us in ways that we don't expect nor fully understand. Whenever we find that what we have is more than our needs – when what we have is a blessing, remind us that every blessing that comes to us may not be for us.

In His name, amen.

Frank L. Ford

TIMES THAT TRY

In the days before the Revolutionary War, Thomas Paine wrote, "These are the times that try men's souls." Those words or similar words could have been spoken in every generation before or since. Those words could well be spoken today. This world never goes very long without wars, or famine, or disease, or something that threatens our lives or our way of life – something that tries our souls.

God knew we would have to live in such a world, and He eased the way for us. Let's pray about it.

Father, in every age the world faces new foes and new fears, but You have not abandoned the world.

In our age, we've seen vast armies of evil empires amassed with terribly destructive weapons as if the world could be wrested from Your control by force. But they discounted Your will and Your power.

Now we see the spawn of evil empires going out in small groups or one-by-one on suicide missions to kill and maim – even children – as if the world could be wrested from Your control by stealth. But they, too, have discounted Your will and Your power.

We understand it is not Your way to make this present world a trouble-free paradise for Your children, but by Your grace, You make it possible for us to live in peace.

A Collection of Prayers

There are so many things and ways we have relied on and taken for granted that now seem to crumble around us like dry leaves.

Our experience and our understanding tell us this is not a time to be at peace, but You are not bound by our experience nor our understanding. You offer peace in a time of turmoil; a peace which passes all understanding.

Father, we are blessed in having a savior who not only cares for our body and our soul but even for our peace of mind as well. He said to all of us when He said to the disciples, "Peace I leave with you; My peace I give you."

Thank you for such a savior. It's in His name we pray. Amen.

Frank L. Ford

TROUBLESOME TIMES

Father, we sing a song with the words, "troublesome times are near." Sometimes it seems that troublesome times are never far away. And though most of our worries never happen, there are very real troubles wherever there are people – at home, at work, at church – everywhere.

We need only to think for a few moments to be so aware of troubles and burdens that we want to cry out. If we take inventory we see broken health, broken vows, broken homes, and broken hearts. We see frustration because of the lack of a sense of direction, and because we can't seem to get ahead and can't go back. We see anxiety because of too little money, too much guilt, too little time, and too much of this world.

It really seems, sometimes, that the writer of Ecclesiastes was exactly right about all of life when he said, "All his days are sorrows; all is vanity and vexation of spirit." All too often we find ourselves wondering, "Why me?" – "Why is this happening?" – "What went wrong?"

For some reason, we persist in the idea that we should understand everything that happens in our lives. We've learned better many times, but still hold to the idea. Help us to learn patience to wait for what You have to work out in our lives. We know that a thousand years in Your sight are but as yesterday when it is past. Help us to adopt an eternity view of life. Help us to see our trials and burdens from the perspective of our lifetime, not just the moment. Help us to remember that many of our past troubles were not as serious as we thought — many, in fact, were not troubles at all, but were for our good later on.

And especially, Father, let us remember to cast our burdens on You and leave them with You to resolve according to Your wisdom and Your will. Having done this, we may be at peace, being assured that a kind, loving, caring Father — who has all wisdom and all power — a friend who said, "Cast your burdens on Me," — is now in control in our hearts as well as in the world.

Help us to be like Job, who while he never found an answer to his suffering, found faith, and said, "Though He slay me, yet will I trust Him."

Father, as we think of others just now, call to our remembrance the burdens upon the hearts of our family, our friends, those at work, at school, those we only hear about.

Thank You, Father, for the power and privilege of prayer.
Thank You for the peace that it affords.
Thank You that it's not limited to times set aside as this time is.
Thank You that this same peace and comfort we feel now can be ours whenever, and from wherever we call upon You.

We praise Your holy name. Amen.

Frank L. Ford

TWO PRAYERS

I have two beautiful prayers to share with you, and mine, between. Bow with me, please.

Open our eyes dear Lord that we may see the far, vast reaches of eternity. Help us to look beyond life's little cares so prone to fret us and the grief that wears our courage thin. Oh may we tune our hearts to Thy great harmony that all the parts may be in perfect sweet accord. Give us Thine own clear vision, blessed Lord.

Father, Sunday is our Sabbath. This is our day for rest and recreation. We play, we nap, and we do chores, if we want. We do a hundred things that we don't do the rest of the week. We use the day to refresh ourselves and seldom stop to think of it as a blessing. We need to be reminded that You rested and created a day of rest for Your children.

Most of us need the rest, not from strenuous physical labor as our fathers and mothers did, but from the stress from pressure that we don't need, can't handle, and can't avoid.

The world we live in and work in is very demanding. It's a spoiled world that wants everything immediately and has largely forgotten common courtesy. If this weren't enough to deal with, we put pressures on ourselves and our loved ones by trying to live up to unreasonable expectations – our own and others.

A Collection of Prayers

Open our eyes that we may see the far vast reaches of eternity. Help us to see over the thick underbrush of this world and its fleeting concerns. Help us to see beyond life's cares.

Father, you've taught us that everything we know, except our soul and the good we do, will perish. We wonder why we act as if this weren't so. The Psalmist said, "His plans endure forever – His purposes last eternally," and yet we remain busy with our plans and our purposes. Tune our hearts to Thy great harmony that all the parts may ever be in perfect, sweet accord.

Father, help us to view life from an eternity point of view. Help us to live out in our lives what we know in our hearts is true.

God, grant me the serenity to accept the things I cannot change, Courage to change the things I can, and wisdom to know the difference. Living one day at a time, enjoying one moment at a time, accepting hardship as the pathway to peace. Taking, as He did, this sinful world as it is, not as I would have it. Trusting that He will make all things right, if I surrender to His will. That I may be reasonably happy in this life, and supremely happy with Him forever in the next.

Hear our prayer, Father. In Jesus name. Amen.

Frank L. Ford

WE BELIEVE

Father, we live in a world so ordered that the time of the rising and setting of the sun and moon can be predicted for years. A world so ordered that after years of dogged research, we barely skim the surface of understanding the world we live in.

We are sometimes so into ourselves that we forget that You not only understand math, and chemistry, and physics, and music, and color, and everything that is, but you understand them because You created them. And this fantastic world is a tiny part of a universe that You created that is so vast that its span is measured in distances that light can travel in years!

We live in a spiritual world, also created by You, that is even more awe-inspiring. And sometimes we are so into ourselves, we ask, "Does God understand how we feel? Does He care?"

Father, forgive our foolishness.

In the physical world, we seek to understand so we may believe. In the spiritual world, we believe so we may understand.

We believe –
We believe that all things work together for good to them that love God.
We believe that if we believe, we shall have everlasting life.
We believe that if we cast our burdens on You, You will sustain us.
We believe that if we forgive, we will be forgiven.

We believe that nothing shall separate us from the love of God. We believe that Jesus is the resurrection and life and whoever believes in Him shall never die.

We believe these things because Your word tells us so, and we believe them because we have lived them.

The world does not understand that faith is as real as a rock, as reliable as the seasons. As Your children, we understand these truths and still sometimes lose sight of them and take our eyes off of You.

Lord, we believe; help our unbelief.

Thank you, Father, for the magnificent opportunity to live in this wondrous world You have made.

Frank L. Ford

WE LIVE BY FAITH

We once lived in a city where there was a school for the blind. We often saw new students on the street walking alone with only their white canes and their faith. Imagine a busy street with cars rushing by, horns blowing, brakes squealing, and no ability to see what was going on – it must have been terrifying.

And we think we live by faith.

We've all lived with people – or worked with people, or worshipped with people who are crippled – that's a harsh, ugly word, but an honest word – people who are crippled in body, but not in spirit – and they keep going, and doing, and smiling.

And we think we live by faith.

When Jesus went to Capernaum, He was approached by a Centurion who said, "Lord, my servant lies at home paralyzed and in terrible suffering." Jesus said, "I will go and heal him." The Centurion replied, "I don't deserve to have You come under my roof. Just say the word, and my servant will be healed."

And we think we live by faith.

For the opening prayer, I want to read a poem by Annie Johnson Flint, with a few words changed. She says what I want to say, but so much better than I can say it.

A Collection of Prayers

I BELIEVE GOD

I believe - but, do I? Am I sure?
Can I trust my trusting to endure?
Can I hope that my belief will last?
Will my hand forever hold You fast?
Am I certain I am saved from sin?
Do I feel Your presence here within?
Do I hear You tell me that You care?
Do I see the answers to my prayers?
Do no fears my confidence assail?
Do I know my faith will never fail?

I believe – yes I do!

I believe You will never fail me, never leave;
I believe You hold me, and I know
Your strong hand will never let me go;
Seeing, hearing, feeling – what are these?
Given or withheld as You shall please.
I believe in You and what You say.
I have faith in You, not in my faith
That may fail, tomorrow or today;
Trust may weaken, feeling pass away,
Thoughts grow weary, anxious or depressed;
I believe in You – and here I rest.

Frank L. Ford

WORSHIP

C.S. Lewis said, "It is the process of being worshipped that God communicates His presence to us." I'd like for us to think about worship for a moment and pray about it.

I like to work crossword puzzles. I remember one in which the clue was "worship." And the answer was "adore." At the time, I didn't think that was the right synonym – but I've since decided that it is the ideal synonym.

We all know what worship is. It's what we're doing now. Worship is singing, praying, reading the bible, praising, having communion, giving, preaching, hearing, and inviting.

If we engage in those things, have we then worshipped? Or, are those things only the elements of worship? I have done the one without having done the other. I confess that I have done all those things and left the building without having worshipped.

When Jesus taught, He used very familiar examples that all of His hearers could not only understand, but identify with. He presented God as a father – "Abba" – which some say is like "Daddy." So in order to better understand God, I can think of my father – or myself, since I am a father. As a father, I know that I always did, and still do, delight in many things with my children, especially things that make them happy and help them.

Jesus said, "If you then, though you are evil, know how to give good gifts to your children, how much more will your Father in heaven give good gifts to those who ask him?" So, to help me understand, God is like me at my very best – only 10,000 times more so.

Some of my happiest moments were when my children brought something broken because they believed I could fix anything – and I fixed it. They were, for the moment, in awe of me and completely receptive to what I had to say. After all, a guy who can fix anything has something on the ball.

Then I made the connection –

When they were in awe of me, they were receptive to me. When I am in awe of God, when I adore Him, I am receptive to Him – I worship Him. We are not commanded to worship Him for His sake. We are commanded to worship Him, to adore Him, so He can bless us.

Let us pray.

Father, these thoughts open our hearts to Jesus' words, "Let the little children come to me, and do not hinder them, for the kingdom of heaven belongs to such as these."

Little children see through child's eyes – capable of being in awe. They do not have the cynic's heart, the jaded mind, the mistrust that so often comes with age and experience.

Help us to see You in our adult years as we saw our mother and father when we were children – as a loving parent who could kiss away tears and pain – and fears that didn't have a name.

Sometimes we long to give up our adulthood and independence that seemed so desirable when we didn't have them, and crawl up on Your lap and have You hold us tight and assure us, as our parents did, that the thunder and lightning, or whatever we saw in our dreams would not harm us.

We repent that we have become wise in the ways of the world. The innocence we gave up is too great a price to have paid.

We realize that innocence lost can't be recaptured. We're left with the problem of needing a child's faith and a sense of awe even though we live in an adult's body with an adult's mind. And we realize this is impossible – without Your help. Once again, we realize that if we will have what we want most, what we want from the greatest depth of our hearts, it is to be had from You and only You – by Your grace.

Help us, just now, to put aside what we know and what we have experienced, and simply adore You – to be in awe of You. Let us hold our tongue and quiet our mind and listen to You. Let us be still and know that You are God and worship You in spirit, in truth, and allow You to communicate Your presence to us.

In Jesus' name.

YOURSELF

God knows what we have need of before we ask, and He does not withhold until we ask. The question comes to mind, Why does He tell us to ask? Why pray?

When we spend time in His presence, we are blessed by it, and the things we came to ask become secondary. So we realize that if we think that prayer is just asking for things, we have missed the point. The point is that our great, loving God is not in the business of granting wishes or "filling orders."

If that were the case, we would be God. When we come to God as He bids us to, God gives Himself.

Let's pray.

Thank you, Father, that in Your wisdom and goodness and love You care less about the desires of our eyes than the desires of our heart. We praise You that You give from Your knowledge of our needs rather than our list of wants.

We learn more of You with our head bowed, our eyes closed, and our mouth shut than in anything else we do.

Frank L. Ford

We come to You as beggars, with no entitlements, no claims on Your vast store of wealth. Everything is Yours. We come asking, and always leave Your presence with more than we thought to ask for.

You give us peace, hope, strength, comfort, understanding, resolve and everything we need for the journey through this world.

But above physical blessings, and even above spiritual blessings, You give of Yourself – and we are filled.

We thank You; we praise You for that.

Amen.

Made in the USA
Las Vegas, NV
19 November 2022